KT-405-232

the Idler book of
CRAP JOBS

100 TALES OF WORKPLACE HELL

Edited by Dan Kieran

BANTAM BOOKS

LONDON • TORONTO • SYDNEY • AUCKLAND • JOHANNESBURG

CRAP JOBS
A BANTAM BOOK: 0 553 81689 6

First publication in Great Britain

PRINTING HISTORY
Bantam edition published 2004

3 5 7 9 10 8 6 4

Bantam Books are published by Transworld Publishers,
61-63 Uxbridge Road, London W5 5SA,
a division of The Random House Group Ltd,
in Australia by Random House Australia (Pty) Ltd,
20 Alfred Street, Milsons Point, Sydney, NSW 2061, Australia,
in New Zealand by Random House New Zealand Ltd,
18 Poland Road, Glenfield, Auckland 10, New Zealand
and in South Africa by Random House (Pty) Ltd,
Endulini, 5a Jubilee Road, Parktown 2193, South Africa.

Papers used by Transworld Publishers are natural, recyclable products made from wood grown in sustainable forests. The manufacturing processes conform to the environmental regulations of the country of origin.

www.booksattransworld.co.uk

You're lucky I turned up. It's just a job, man.

Bill Hicks

Compiled and Edited by
Dan Kieran

Designed by
Gavin Pretor-Pinney and Sonia Ortiz Alcón

Illustrations by
Gwyn

Photographs by
Rachel Poulton

Acknowledgements and thanks:

Simon Benham, Brenda Kimber, Patrick Janson-Smith, Judith Welsh, Alison Tulett,
Chris Yates, John Lloyd, Kevin Parr, Henry Littlechild, Ben Hassett, Kevin Kieran,
Jill Kieran, Gareth Kieran, Rita Kieran, John Kieran, Molly Smith, Roger Halton,
Judy Munday, Ben Munday, Kit Munday, Nick Munday, Richard Munday, Hugh Breton,
Jo Mayer, Kieran Topping, Jamie Dwelly, Pat Dennison, Mr Chittock, Colin Charde,
Tom Espley, Ken Mackinnon, John Potter, Lawrence Pointer, John Frusciante,
Paul Hamilton, Tony Husband, Edward Sage, Clare Pollard, Victoria Hull, Will Hogan,
Matthew De Abaitua, John Nicholson, Mathew Clayton, The Three Bills, John Dwelly,
Stephen Armstrong, Glenn Robert, Finlay Coutts-Britton and Mimi Poulton.

CRAP JOBS CONTENTS

WITH A VERY FEW EXCEPTIONS, the world of jobs is characterized by stifling boredom, grinding tedium, poverty, petty jealousies, sexual harassment, loneliness, deranged co-workers, bullying bosses, seething resentment, illness, exploitation, stress, helplessness, hellish commutes, humiliation, depression, appalling ethics, physical fatigue and mental exhaustion. But tales of woe can make for hilarious reading and it is with this in mind that we have compiled one hundred accounts of workplace hell.

For over ten years, *The Idler* has provided a home for the disgruntled, disillusioned and dismayed, and all the stories have been sent in to *The Idler*'s website by our readers and contributors. They will make you laugh and they will make you cry.

We've also gathered various shocking statistics relating to the daily grind. And we have trawled the archives and found some of the worst jobs from the last three hundred years. These we have called 'Ye Olde Crappe Jobs'.

Overall it's a revealing snapshot of the Western World of Work, and the vast gap between what jobs promise and what they deliver.

Low low wages, corporate crap, rubbish products, nasty stains and dim-witted bosses: the glorious fruits of the Industrial Revolution are all here.

Tom Hodgkinson, Editor of The Idler

100 MODEL

Hours:
10am-10pm
Wages:
£25 per job

HUMILIATING,
DISGUSTING

Modelling isn't all coke and catwalks, you know. If you want someone with an enormous beard and you'd like to splat their beard with a custard pie for a kids TV programme, then you'd call my agency who'd call me.

The custard and the chidren were bad enough, I'd grown thick skinned about such humiliation over the years, but you would have thought they'd let me wash before kicking me out of the studio. When I finally made it to the station, at the peak of the summer rush hour, my congealed, putrid beard was beginning to smell. I got on to my train, with sweaty, grim-faced commuters, for the half-hour journey home. After ten minutes we stopped. Three motionless hours later the stench was medieval.

ANON

IDENTITY HAS BEEN
CONCEALED TO PROTECT
THE HUMILIATED

99 HOSPITAL BED SALESMAN

Hours:
8am-7pm
Wages:
£6.50 per hour

HUMILIATING, SOUL-DESTROYING

I worked as a salesman for a company selling hospital beds in South London. The sales side was OK, the hospital staff, despite being wigged out with exhaustion and stress, still managed to smile and be receptive to my orthopaedic mattresses sales pitch. But the targets set for us by our slick managers were stupefyingly unrealistic and the penalties for failing to meet them insidiously cruel.

Every Friday evening we all trudged back to the office, a fifth-floor seventies tower block, to go through the sales records for that week. Whoever had sold the fewest mattresses had to suffer the weekly humiliation in front of everyone else in the company.

The terror of those moments still haunts me. One grey, drizzling winter afternoon it was my turn. I was ordered to strip down to my pants and run round the car park five storeys below while my co-workers shouted and screamed at me through the windows. Obviously any sane person would have told them to fuck off and quit there and then. That's any sane person without a mortgage and family depending on their income.

Then one Christmas the boss hired a restaurant for our Yuletide bash. The four salesmen who hadn't reached their annual targets were 'slaves' for the evening to the twelve who had. We had to wait on them all night, pay for their drinks and serve their food. Even I managed to quit after that.

JACK

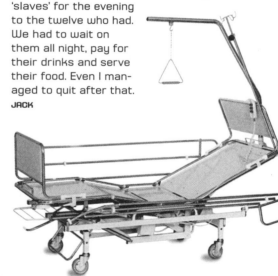

9

98 BANK CLERK

Hours:
8.30am-5.30pm
Wages:
£3.80 per hour

SOUL-DESTROYING

Working as a cashier has many disadvantages. The pay, the hours and the slow decline into alcoholism that you endure to compensate for the unrelenting misery, to mention but a few. But worst of all were the 'mystery shoppers' who spot-checked us to ensure we followed set procedures when serving. We all had a list Sellotaped to our tills: 'Greet the customer. Make eye-contact. Use the customer's name. SMILE. Say goodbye. SMILE. Don't distance yourself from the bank if the customer has a complaint.' etc. My Team Leader told me during my 'Performance Cascade' that any score below 97% would be a total failure. A month later she thrust a piece of paper at me with a scowl on her face. She was going crimson as I read the last line, 'When I asked for mortgage advice Dan told me, "The banks just rip you off with terrible interest rates. Try a Building Society instead." Overall Score - 58%.' Apparently I'd let the whole branch down.

DAN KIERAN

UNRELENTING MISERY

RACHEL POULTON

WORK KILLS

Your job could kill you. Recent figures released by the United Nations claim that worldwide, work kills more than two million people every year. That's equivalent to a September 11 disaster every day, and far outstrips the 650,000 who are killed each year by war. The figure for deaths from work-related accidents or disease are also three times as great as the number killed each year by drugs and alcohol combined.

CRAP JOB TRIVIA

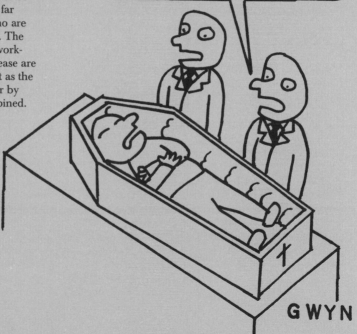

97 TRAFFIC COUNTER

Hours:
8am-8pm
Wages:
£5 per hour

HUMILIATING

I did traffic counting one very long day a couple of years ago. It was autumn and I had to be in Deptford – miles away from where I lived – at 8am. I knew the bus journey would take hours so I had to get up ridiculously early. When the alarm clock rang it was pitch black outside and when I left the house it began drizzling and got steadily worse. When I got to Deptford the rain came at me like the arrows at Agincourt and my socks quickly became sodden. Our traffic-counting team leader, a burly weather-beaten man, grinned heartily as he shook my hand, the rain streaming off his beard. He looked like an Icelandic fishing-boat captain. He was in his element.

I was packed off with a clipboard and pencil, and a little yellow thing with a button that clocked up traffic. I was positioned outside a school for the next twelve hours and it rained pretty much the whole time. I watched for cars and motorcycles and lorries and pedestrians crossing the road and marked them off on my checklist. The team leader visited me every hour on his rounds, which prevented me from buggering off down the pub.

The only shelter was a tree and I huddled there until the first school break when hundreds of urchins poured out and decided that I was the most fascinating thing they'd ever seen. I had to answer the same question – subtle variations of, 'What are you doing?' – all day until the last little shit had gone home. I attempted to conceal myself from them but it proved difficult as I was wearing a bright yellow safety jacket.

The only relief came when I went on my breaks. I sat completely drenched in a dingy pie and mash shop for an hour at lunch, contemplating the hellish afternoon ahead, and in a pub for an hour at dinner time, contemplating whether I should jack it in and go straight home or stand around until 8. I wish I had gone home.

EDWARD SAGE

ONE THOUSAND FIVE HUNDRED AND
SEVENTY-SIX, ONE THOUSAND FIVE
HUNDRED AND SEVENTY-SEVEN

'OUR HIGHLY TRAINED CHEFS PREPARE THE
FINEST ITALIAN SAUCES TO PROVIDE YOU
WITH AN AUTHENTIC TASTE OF TUSCANY'

96 KITCHEN PORTER

Hours:
5am-midnight
Wages:
£1.80 per hour

 HUMILIATING

Back in the late eighties, there was a chain of pasta places whose gimmick was that you could eat as much as you liked for something like three quid. As a student, I had dined there a few times and found it to be rather good, or at least edible.

So when my local branch put a plea via the Job Centre for kitchen porters, I thought it sounded great. They said that if you did well you could soon graduate to sous-chef.

On my first day I found out why the place was so cheap: the staff were crap and the food was crap. The whole process had been de-skilled beyond belief. Up in the sweltering kitchen, I had to do the washing up and send down sauces to the chef, who then heated them in a bain-marie.

There was a dumb waiter and I communicated with the chef via a dodgy intercom. After seven minutes' training from the weaselly manager, I was left on my own. The plates started coming. I rinsed them and shoved them into a giant washing-up machine. The rubber gloves were full of holes and I scorched my hands. While the machine was on, I ran to the cold-store and pulled out a large plastic bag of pre-prepared sauce. Each bag had a name tag on it, 'peasant', 'romero', 'cheese', 'napoletana' and a few others.

The idea was to keep one of each submerged in a giant cauldron of boiling water.

When the chef ran out of a particular sauce, he would order top-ups from me. The intercom didn't work too well and he would shout: 'wam bam!' 'What?' I would answer. 'WAM BAM!' he would shout. 'What?' I would say again, panicking. 'PEASANT!' he would holler in a state of great agitation. I would run to the cauldron, look at the name tags and find that there was no peasant.

Now I would run to the cold-store, pull out of a bag of peasant, hold it over a plastic container and slice it open like a pig's bladder. The pre-made sauce would tumble into the box and then I'd bung it in the microwave before sending it downstairs.

I also had to make the lasagne and the apple pie in the giant industrial ovens. Inevitably I would burn them and have to start again, occasioning more abuse from the chef downstairs.

I imagined that they and the waiters, miles above me in the restaurant's hierarchy, were having a whale of a time downstairs with the customers. Occasionally the manager would wander in and tell me to get a move on. I would ask for new rubber gloves but none ever came.

I would be literally dripping in sweat. Finally, the shift would end and the bains-marie would come up to be washed. While I scrubbed away at the caked-on sauces, everybody else would have a beer downstairs and then bugger off home before I could get down to join them. A couple of nights I got my best friend in to help, which made it more bearable but otherwise I was alone.

When I finally got my payslips, I found that I had only been paid till midnight, even though I was often washing up till one. I felt righteously exploited but I was powerless to do much about it.

TOM HODGKINSON

95 JOURNALIST

Hours:
10am-6pm
Wages:
£7 per hour

HUMILIATING,
FUTILE

Desperately keen to get on to the journalistic career ladder, I found myself working for £50 a day (before tax) for the magazine supplement of a well-known tabloid Sunday magazine. The boss was one of those terrifying people who keep you on a piece of elastic. You think they've finished telling you off because they have gone quiet, so you gingerly begin to retreat to your desk. Then suddenly they will pipe up again, and you will move forwards to receive yet more humiliation at close quarters. 'This is the sloppiest piece of journalism I have ever read,' she said once when I showed her some research I had done on Dawn French from the cuttings library, before sending me out to the garage to pick up her car. But truth never came near the magazine. It was pure sex and celebs, diets and Russell Grant. For example, she decided she wanted an interview with Nirvana, which would have been great for me. But she had this idea that Nirvana were a real-life version of *Wayne's World*, and however much I tried to disabuse her of this notion she stuck to it. Thankfully there was no way Nirvana wanted to be in this magazine so I never had to face Kurt Cobain with the question: 'So tell me, Kurt, about how you got your idea for the band from *Wayne's World*.' Another editor there, one of the coke-snorting, work-experience-girl-abusing blokes, accused me of stealing because I had accepted a free bottle of wine from a PR (one of my jobs was to check the price of wine for the wine column) and threatened to sack me. I would sit at my desk fuming and inventing my resignation speech but my reveries would be interrupted by another editor who would come over to me, rattling her purse and chirruping: 'Coffee run? Coffee run?'

The highlight of the week would be writing the 'hilarious' captions for the celeb pics at the front of the mag. I dreaded every day and was permanently skint. For some reason I submitted myself to this torture for two years before I was luckily sacked. It was around four years before I could bear to visit that part of town again.

ANON

LONDON'S FLEET STREET

17

94 DETERGENT SALESMAN

Hours:
8.30am-4.30pm
Wages:
Av. £15 per day

HUMILIATING,
IMMORAL, DANGEROUS

I once did the door-to-door household goods thing. I worked twelve hours a day, six days a week, and was expected to do 'Spazzing'. This involved pretending to be mentally handicapped to gain sympathy at the door. Yes, I know... But imagine how desperate I must have been to take the job in the first place.

We were dropped off and picked up by the boss who drove a minibus. Whoever made the least money each day would have to sit in the 'Slap Seat' and be beaten by the others on the way home. Some people had worked there so long that they began to behave as though they really were mentally handicapped.
DAN SMITH

93 DIY STORE STOCK-TAKER

Hours:
8pm-9am
Wages:
£5 per hour

HUMILIATING,
FUTILE

After twenty years of getting away with it, as a 'self-employed' artist, craftsperson, stallholder, occasional community arts worker, and uninsured removal man for the needy, I was back to the world of the crap job. I grabbed a one-night stand offered by an agency: overnight stock-taking, at a DIY store in Cardiff. Coaches would be laid on from North Devon. Travelling time unpaid, five quid an hour, maybe twelve hours' work. It sounded crap, but poverty was the deciding factor.

I was required to attend an hour's unpaid training, in the art of using a little bleeping scanner and make a promise not to tell anyone that I was just a temp, and not a highly trained employee of the stock-taking contractor.

On arrival after the three-hour coach drive, we were allocated numbers, letters, teams and a supervisor, a mixed breed of painfully enthusiastic team coaches, patient cynics, spiteful nags and Nazi thugs.

We were out to hunt barcodes. At breakneck speed, several hundred of us, zapping them with our little rayguns, a horde of bleeping locusts, working according to a divine plan we could only dimly perceive. We were team players. Speed was good and mistakes were bad.

Bill from Glasgow was an old pro at this sort of thing. 'Go slow,' he told me. 'Don't knacker yourself, more hours equals more dosh.'

But troublemakers were weeded out, sacked on the spot, confined to the staff canteen, and held under the eye of a security guard until home time.

Ten-minute coffee breaks were reduced to three by the journey through the vast consumerist cathedral. At three in the morning, I was on my knees under filthy display fitments in my nice white shirt, shifting filthy fucking quarry tiles while a mate on another team was out in the pissing rain counting tasteless garden ornaments. I listened to the automatic announcements to long-vanished shoppers telling them of the joys of the restaurant.

Grudgingly I did a couple more nights, but seaside ice-cream selling beckoned. There was no contest.

PETE LOVEDAY

92 CHICKEN INSPECTOR

Hours:
8am-4pm
Wages:
£2.74 per hour

DISGUSTING, IMMORAL

Chicken farming is a very Fordist business. It has very little in common with the sweet, rustic and rural image many of us have of farming. The 'farm' I was misfortunate enough to slave at consisted of several large sheds filled with cages that maybe had twenty or thirty chickens in an area a little over a metre square. There were maybe 500+ such cages on the site. My grimmest job was patrolling and inspecting the chickens. If a chicken became lame, its cage-mates would start pecking it and if not stopped would peck their erstwhile colleague to death. My job was to remove the lame bird from the cage and ring its neck. This was never an easy task - frequently I over-wrung the wretched beast's neck in a vain effort to reduce post-death spasms. All this left me with was a still spasming headless body in one hand, and a small and quite pissed-off looking chicken's head in the other.

Perhaps inevitably I started to do my rounds less than diligently - letting cannibalization take its course seemed somehow preferable to my incompetent and gruesome methods.

DAVID EVANS

Ye Olde Crappe Job: 18th-CENTURY MINER, 1753

From *A Vindication of Natural Society*, 1753, by Edmund Burke

I suppose in Great Britain upwards of an hundred thousand people are employed in lead, tin, iron, copper, and coal mines; these unhappy wretches scarce ever see the light of the sun; they are buried in the bowels of the earth; there they work at a severe and dismal task, without the least prospect of being delivered from it; they subsist upon the coarsest and worst sort of fare; they have their health miserably impaired, and their lives cut short, by being perpetually confined in the close vapour of these malignant minerals. An hundred thousand more at least are tortured without remission by the suffocating smoke, intense fires, and constant drudgery necessary in refining and managing the products of those mines.

91 FACTORY WORKER

Hours:
8.30am-4.30pm
Wages:
£1.90 per hour

DISGUSTING

One summer I went to Guernsey and got a job working in a factory that made medical equipment. My job was to pick out any defective pieces. Everything was colour coded by disease, blue for heart disease, green for cancer and it being the early nineties when everyone was a bit ignorant the dreaded purple was for AIDS.

Because I had been to college everyone called me 'the dropout', and maybe because of this I was befriended by an addled hippie called Dennis. His penchant for Special Brew and LSD often meant he wouldn't bother coming in for days at a time, but when he did the job suddenly became bearable. His speciality was sticker jokes. He would wander round the factory covertly putting stickers on people's backs with messages written on them, 'Cock For Sale' or 'Gender Bender'. My favourite was a sticker he put on one of the old ladies, it had an arrow pointing towards her head and underneath said, 'Vacant Lot for Sale (Never been used).'

Whenever I see Guernsey on the TV I think fondly of Dennis and hope there is someone in the factory right now walking round with a sticker on their back that says, 'I will wank you off this lunchtime.' **MATHEW CLAYTON**

90 CRAP CRISP CHUCKER

Hours:
3pm-11pm
Wages:
£5 per hour

DISGUSTING,
SOUL-DESTROYING

In a futile attempt to finance my second year of film school, I had heard about possible summer employment in the 'quality control' division of a crisp factory. It was a five-minute drive from my house, full-time hours, and it paid 50p above the minimum wage. I wasn't exactly sure what it entailed, but what the hell - how bad could it be? I signed up and was hired on the spot.

Ten minutes later my immediate supervisor (later to be affectionately nicknamed 'The Dragon Bitch') delivered me to a room that could only be described as a Human Oven. It was then that I came to the grim realization that the entire job consisted of standing (and sweating) in front of a very large conveyor belt for the entire eight-hour shift. With my

GWYN

well-manicured bare hands, I was required to dispose of all the blemished, newly cut, deep-fryer-hot potato crisps that whizzed by at Warp 9, while the heavy, oily steam that emanated from the conveyer belt found refuge in my open, teenage pores. If there was a black or green spot on a chip, it had to go. I

didn't wear gloves, I didn't wear a hair net, and I wasn't even required to wash my hands (or turn my head when I felt the urge to cough or sneeze). Think about THAT the next time you pop open a bag to serve at a party.

We got three ten-minute breaks, and thirty minutes for lunch. Nine times out of ten, my lunch got lifted from the fridge, so I'd be forced to drink the warm, stale water from the factory tap instead.

On top of everything else, as the shifts were either from 7am-3pm or from 3pm-11pm, I had absolutely no life. Having said that, the primary contributor to my massive unpopularity that summer is more likely to have stemmed from the fact that I constantly emitted the distinct odour of deep-fried flesh.

I only lasted six weeks.

SARAH JANES

CRAP JOB TRIVIA

WORKED UP
Full-time employees in the UK work an average of 43.5 hours a week, the longest hours in Europe. In France they work an average of 38.2 and in Germany 39.9. According to TUC figures, both France and Germany are far more productive than the UK.

89 AERIAL PHOTOGRAPH SELLER

Hours:
7.30am-5.30pm
Wages:
80p per hour

HUMILIATING, FUTILE

The deal was that me and three other doley/studenty types were picked up in an estate car early one morning in the Hyde Park area of Leeds by an oily 'controller'. On the journey over the Pennines he assured us that skilled practitioners of this game could expect to take a ton or more home in our back pockets at the end of each day. The kingsize photographs covered sections of around forty houses of new Barratt-style estates on the outskirts of the Lancashire town. Taken from a helicopter on an 'unusually bright and clear summer's day', these items – at £20 a pop, including 'luxury, clip-frame' – would be a 'joy and delight for ever'. Of this £20 we intrepid salesmen, vendors of happiness to the good people of Wigan, would receive a £4 share.

After my first day of conscientiously picking

out each house from the photograph before approaching the door ready to vomit my spiel at the unsuspecting occupier I had sold a total of two aerial photographs. The first was to a young family whose daughter could be seen, very blurred, riding her bike in the front garden, and the second to a comic pair of middle-aged homosexuals who answered the door in tight-black speedos and who could be seen on their photograph clearly sunbathing in the same get-up.

On the way back our still oily controller insisted on stopping off at a rotten country boozer to celebrate our day's takings. By the time I arrived home late into the evening my hard-earned £8 had long evaporated into the ether. Not good as I'd only taken the work because I was really desperate for money. The joy I felt at securing myself employment on the Vaseline Intensive Care production line at a factory in Seacroft some two weeks later was not entirely ironic.

ROSS HOLLOWAY

88 INDUSTRIAL CLEANER

Hours:
8am-6pm
Wages:
Didn't get
paid

HUMILIATING, FUTILE,
DISGUSTING, DANGEROUS

In a litany of crap jobs I have had, my time with a company that cleaned shopping trollies stands out like a gangrenous, pus-filled thumb.

The job, advertised as an 'apprenticeship', turned out to be a clean-up, or rather cover-up, job for a company whose premises had just been condemned by health and safety inspectors.

They needed the place made presentable for the inspectors' return, I needed the £20 a day, cash, no questions.

My first inkling that I and the other unemployable youth they assigned to work alongside me might have made a mistake was when the liquid that dripped on my legs as I carried a box from one overcrowded store room to another burnt several large holes in my jeans.

When I found myself standing 30 feet up a scaffolding platform just in front of a sign saying, 'Do not climb on this structure' handing down to my colleague a split bag of white chemical powder marked, 'Do not handle without protective clothing and breathing apparatus', my fears crystalized, much like my lungs probably will before I reach forty.

The next part of my job was to paint the toilet. It wouldn't have been so bad if the toilet had not been a cramped airless room and the paint the same as that used to mark yellow lines on the road. I have taken some dodgy pills and some weird trips during my ill-spent life but none of them can compare to the effect of breathing in the concentrated fumes of that toxic paint. When I found that the job was going no quicker despite the fact I clearly had three pairs of hands, I handed the paint to my workmate and walked out. Now that's what I call getting high on pot.

But despite the fact my life-span has probably been reduced by twenty years, that I developed an unhealthy addiction to paint fumes, and that those jeans cost me half my illegally claimed dole that week, the job was my crappest for one reason alone.

Despite our best efforts, the inspectors returned and closed the place down. Before we were paid.

The bastards.

JAKE HADLEE

87 TV COMPANY RUNNER

Hours:
9.30am-7pm
Wages:
A three-zone travelcard

DISGUSTING

A few years ago I worked as a runner for a TV company in Soho. Despite hoping to learn the tricks of the trade I ended up spening most of my time doing menial office crap. One day the management decided to move all the long-term files from the attic into the basement, so we crawled into this tiny, dusty space, picked up the boxes, which invariably decomposed on contact, and shifted twenty years' worth of VAT forms to the newly done-up basement four storeys below. After two weeks everything was sorted. The building looked respectable, all the files were where they should have been and we were proud(ish) of a job well done.

Two days later the sewer under the basement burst, clogged by the grease from the chip shop next door, and our brand-new archive was flooded with raw sewage. We donned wellies, masks and gloves and waded in to rescue the sodden files, fighting the constant urge to puke from the revolting smell. We had to use brooms to keep the six-inch-deep tide of shit away. None of us could stand to be in the room for more than five minutes, and it took us five days to get everything out.

ANON

86 KEBAB SHOP ASSISTANT

Hours:
4am-12pm
Wages:
£4.40 per hour

DISGUSTING

Shivering in a shed behind the shop, my unenviable task was to assemble the meat.

It's brain-numbingly simple and hand-numbingly cold. You take about 10kg of defrosting lamb mince and mix it with 'secret ingredients' (spices, salt, pepper and volume increasing 'grit'). Then you grab a huge handful of the freezing mixture, form it into a dough-nut shape and then push it over a three-foot pole that is welded to a metal base. You repeat this process until you've built up a disgusting tower of raw flesh on the pole before shaping it with your hands, like a potter creates a pot, into that traditional 'ele-phant leg' shape you see revolving slowly in grease pits across the country.

HERE'S ONE I MADE EARLIER

I did this for eight hours, plunging my hands into the cold, slimy, fatty raw mince, shaping the clammy towers of meat and increasingly feeling sick because of the constant smell of lamb blood and spices.

TOM STAINER

85 TRUCK PAINTER

Hours:
8.45am-6pm
Wages:
£2.75 per hour

HUMILIATING

I once had a summer job in the garages of a national delivery company. My job was the annual repainting of little delivery trucks that went round the warehouse carrying parcels on a sort of giant scalextric track. My boss appeared to be as thick as two short planks. I blame the paint fumes he'd been inhaling for years. He'd simply stand behind me, or more often sit in an old armchair he'd salvaged from somewhere, and regale me with tales that sounded like complete bullshit. Finally, one day, he proudly announced that he'd been awarded the Purple Heart medal for bravery. Now, even a wet-behind-the-ears kid like me knew that the Purple Heart is an American service medal, and isn't given to non-Americans. I promptly threw down my paintbrush and turned on him, telling him I was sick of all his whining bullshit and why didn't he just fuck off and let me do the job in peace. He looked very hurt, and quietly retired, leaving me feeling a mixture of self-pride for my courage, and a twinge of guilt for hurting the old git's feelings. He was harmless, after all...

The next day he came over to me, and without a word, handed me a small package wrapped in tissue. Inside was a little box, which contained, of course, a Purple Heart medal, together with a letter of commendation, and an old photo of three Army guys in the jungle.

Turns out he was in the Korean War, one of a small team whose job it was to sneak past enemy snipers and booby traps, worm their way into hollowed-out underground bunkers the enemy had built, set mines, then get the hell out before it blew. Every mission was considered a suicide mission, and it's a miracle any of them ever came back. He was one of only three British service-men ever to be awarded the Purple Heart.

ROB
TAYLOR

84 MAGGOT FARMER

Hours:
9am-6pm
Wages:
£2.20 per hour

DISGUSTING

Working in a maggot farm has to be the worst job I've ever done. Fortunately it was over ten years ago, so the smell has now left my nostrils.

In a beautiful corner of the Cambridgeshire countryside there is a farm. But unlike most farms it has no cows and no sheep, only maggots. I spent my first day in the 'worm pit', which was like an Olympic swimming pool filled with the rotting carcasses of animals and fish pieces that the maggots lived in/on. I had waders and was instructed to walk in and turn the flesh over periodically. Once you've got the hang of that you're then given a sort of promotion and the 'fly room' beckons. The fly room turned out to be a hangar-sized area sealed by

netting that housed more flies than you could ever imagine. Big flies too, which were purposefully kept for breeding. Stud flies if you will. The noise was unreal. It was like being stuck in some kind of horror film or Stephen King's imagination!

CRISTIAN

83 DUSTMAN

Hours:
6am-1pm / 3pm-10pm
Wages:
£3.50 per hour

DISGUSTING

The winter of '93 was to be a long one. Spat out of university the previous summer I returned to the provincial hell of my hometown and the ignominy of my childhood bedroom.

The mornings passed swiftly enough. I'd roll up at the council yard just before 6am with the other local outcasts (including my best mate) for whichever bin round happened to be a man down. Eventually we even secured a permanent position on round four (our local round), which meant I was lucky enough to clear the rubbish from my own house, much to the neighbours' delight and the pride of my parents.

We'd jog behind the dustcart to the pre-piled mini mountains of rubbish, occasionally trying to trip each other over, vying for the best position to chuck the black bags in the back of the 'wagon'. Our pervert driver meanwhile would leaf through some of the choicer periodicals

found on our travels, smoke fags, and occasionally leap out to piss down the side of the cart.

Our favourite pastime didn't have a name. We'd both hold back a bag, usually a fairly light, non-black bag, the type you get in a pedal bin or from the supermarket. We'd signal the driver to move on (there was a bell in the cabin), set the hopper in motion (the thing that crushes the rubbish) and then wait. Whoever threw last won, provided that his bag made the back of the wagon. Needless to say bag selection became crucial. A miss could be catastrophic. If you've never seen a bag of used sanitary towels explode on the public highway you haven't lived.

We'd be finished by about 1pm and then my friend and I would treat the neighbours and our proud mothers to an exhibition of our footie skills in either his road or mine until it was time for Richard Whiteley and Carol Vorderman to test our word skills.

I've just bashed this out from my desk in a trendy company in East London, and am now listening to the company director's old Etonian voice rebounding around the former warehouse, bollocking some bloke with a Hoxton fin. I reflect that during those six months I met some of the most genuine, contented people you could ever wish to spend time with.

JAMES BURNHAM

CRAP JOB TRIVIA

DEATH FROM OVERWORK

According to the DTI 16% of full-time employees in the UK work over sixty hours a week. This takes them into what is known in Japan as the Karoshi zone. Karoshi, which means death from overwork, is such a serious problem that the Japanese Government pay out compensation to the victim's family in every confirmed case.

TIME WAS MONEY

GWYN

82 HOLIDAY CAMP WAITER

Hours:
45hrs per week
Wages:
£1.22 per hour
plus full board

DANGEROUS

The worst job I ever had was when I worked as a waiter at a holiday camp in North Wales. Aside from the dreadful wages, crap food and Third World living conditions in the chalets (two rooms, one plug, no kitchen, toilet or sink), perhaps the worst thing about it was Scouse Week.

This was actually a fortnight when the impoverished and violent citizens of not just Liverpool, but also Manchester and Birmingham, would descend on the place because they were offered cheap holidays. Seems like a good idea but the problem was that if they saw anyone in one of the camp's uniforms they would attack them. This was because most of them were aware that we couldn't retaliate because if you had any sort of a mark on you, you'd be sacked. Every single day members of staff ran the gauntlet of insane, drunk and violent scousers, and tried hard to avoid getting battered. By the end of this fortnight half the staff in the restaurants had been sacked for the heinous crime of getting attacked by scallies and having the bruises to show for it. The staff also got fed whatever crap was left over from the restaurants the customers were fed in, so we were frequently offered a choice of hamburgers, chicken burgers or veggie burgers. If you had the temerity to complain, you'd be barred from the staff canteen and when your wage was only £55 a week, this made it nigh on impossible to feed yourself.

BRIAN McCLUSKEY

RED COLLAR WORKERS

33

81 TAMPON FACTORY CLEANER

Hours:
8.45am-5.45pm
Wages:
£2.30 per hour

DISGUSTING

The summer holidays of 1980 were not generally memorable for me and by and large they are lost in a fog of teenage drunken disorderliness. The only clear recollection I have of that time is the two weeks spent cleaning a tampon factory in Hampshire.

While the full-time staff took their summer holidays, for a princely £2.30 an hour, I swept, sucked, pushed and prised the world's favourite tampon from every orifice in the building. Down the sides of huge compressors, beneath the never-ending conveyor belts, hanging tenuously from vast fluorescent strip lights, their little tails waving gently in the breeze - was there nowhere these little critters couldn't get to?

I could only presume that some kind of tampon tennis game had been developed by the bored workers.

Supervision was slack to say the least and as the days wore on I became less diligent and took to sleeping off my hangovers in the toilet.

Waking from one of my snoozes to go on tea break, I spun at full speed down the spiral staircase towards what I thought was a pair of

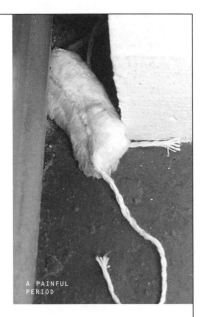
A PAINFUL PERIOD

automatic sliding doors. Unfortunately I misjudged my aim somewhat and smashed into the full-length glass panel next to the sliding doors, shattering it completely. By some miracle, and to the disbelief of a gathering crowd, I escaped totally unscathed.

MARK WATERFIELD

80 AQUARIUM CASHIER

Hours: 10am-6pm
Wages: £3.30 per hour

HUMILIATING

One summer I worked on the ticket desk at an aquarium. There were three ticket staff and about nine managers, who worked in an adjoining office that had a one-way mirrored window overlooking our desk. We were under constant surveillance through the one-way mirror and if the managers saw us talking, chewing or removing our regulation red baseball caps, they would ring through on the internal phone to tell us off (ie; 'We can see you chewing. Please remove whatever you have in your mouth'). It was worse than being back at school.

Each day a manager would assign one of us to 'Sammy the Seal' duty. This involved dressing up in an enormous rubber seal suit, which had two-foot-long red clown shoes and a pumpkin-shaped head. 'Sammy' would be required to lumber up and down the seafront handing out flyers and then 'entertain' the children's parties with games of 'Sammy the Seal Says'.

'Sammy the Seal' duty was meted out as punishment for whoever was out of favour with the managers that day. Being especially unpopular for my repeated non-cap-wearing offences and because of my inability to grin inanely at the general public, I was often ordered to don the rubber suit. That summer was very hot, which made the suit incredibly sweaty and uncomfortable. The head in particular smelt of rancid feet.

Handing out flyers, though dull and tiring, did at least allow you to escape the perpetual Big Brother scrutiny of the managers. But entertaining the children was ghastly. Under the instruction of Donald, a 'resting' actor, you had to execute a torturous routine of, 'Sammy says touch your toes', 'Sammy says clap your hands', 'Sammy says' etc, *ad nauseam*. The kids were not fooled by the seal outfit - in a sugar-fuelled frenzy they would attack you from all sides, tunelling their hands underneath the suit in order to pinch you and scream, 'It's not really a seal, there's a lady in there, I can feel a lady.' Sammy was supposed to remain mute but I frequently told them to 'Fuck off', which prompted screams of 'Sammy the Seal said a rude word.'

ROWENA MACDONALD

79 GLASS COLLECTOR

Hours:
7pm-4am
Wages:
£5.75 per hour

HUMILIATING,
DISGUSTING

The ad asked for a 'glass collector' in a local club so off I went. I soon discovered I was the only girl glass collector, which meant that whatever went on in the club that related to women I was left to deal with. The main area was the women's hell hole of a toilet.

When a girl drops her bottle down the toilet it naturally blocks, when you're out on the piss and it's not your toilet you just don't care... so as you can imagine it would start off blocked... then a layer of sick, shit and fag butts would all pile on top.

Who was the mug who had to take the bottle out? Me. And what with? A black plastic bag so you could feel every nook and cranny down there.

To add to the joy there was once a flood in the main toilet and I had to spend the whole night in my flimsy shoes, ankle-high in toilet water with a rather large Hoover sucking up the continuous fountain of water coming up from the floor. There were so many awful things about working in this club: being sleazed at by weird drunken guys, stepped on, pushed by morons who couldn't dance, the constant smell of sick, scooping girls up from the toilet floors. God forbid that I ever get subjected to that again or any other poor soul.

JULIA GLENDINNING

BUNCH OF GLASS

78 WAREHOUSE ASSISTANT

Hours:
8am-6pm
Wages:
£4.50 per hour

DANGEROUS

When I arrived for my first day I was met by the manager at reception who issued me with a clocking-in card and personal locker. He then introduced me to the staff on the swelteringly hot factory floor. That first week I worked alongside three blokes which we shall call Wayne, Reg and Ron.

Wayne was in his mid-thirties and had a penchant for showing everybody his 'sweaty back wheels', or 'Daryl Halls' through two holes in his jean pockets. Reg was in his early fifties and was just an out-and-out filthy bastard. His locker was a shrine to the *Daily Sport* and Readers' Wives. I later learnt that in their spare time Wayne and Reg were part of a firm of armed robbers. Ron was an old pisshead who always slipped a quarter bottle of vodka meths into his big bottle of Tizer after lunch. He was pleasant enough to me, but I certainly wouldn't have left him alone with a small child.

Our duties consisted of cutting out perforated cardboard displays of the *Titanic* film for use in video stores with the aid of a home-made chisel or 'digger' as Ron fondly called his. Ron was kind enough to lend me one of his 'diggers' but unfortunately I snapped it on the second day and he didn't speak to me for a week.

Wayne and Reg invited me to the local pub to watch an England game. I explained to them that I couldn't make it as I had another job in an off-licence in the evenings. The next morning in the canteen both Wayne and Reg approached me:

'All right, Sweaty! [My nick name was Sweaty Sock Jock on account of my Scottish ancestry.] Tell us about this other job of yours.'

The penny suddenly dropped.

'What's the security like in your shop? What if we both came in late one night with a couple of ski masks on and a shooter and done the till over? There would be something in it for you, of course, but we might have to rough you up a bit to make it look believable.'

PATER SONNEUM

Ye Olde Crappe Job: VICTORIAN SERVANT, 1860

From the diary of Hannah Cullwick, 27, general servant, 1860

Swept & dusted the rooms and the hall. Laid the hearth & got breakfast up. Clean'd 2 pairs of boots. Made the beds & emptied the slops. Clean'd and washed the breakfast things up. Clean'd the plate; clean'd the knives & got dinner up. Clean'd the kitchen up; unpack'd a hamper. Clean'd the steps & flags on my knees. Blackleaded the scraper in front of the house; clean'd the street flags too on my knees. Wash'd up in the scullery. Clean'd the pantry on my knees... Scrubbed the flags around my house & clean'd the window sills. Clean'd the privy & scullery floor on my knees. Wash'd the dog & clean'd the sinks down. Put the supper ready for Ann to take up, for I was too dirty & tired to go upstairs.

77 MAINTENANCE FITTER

Hours:
8am-5.30pm
Wages:
£7.90 per hour

DISGUSTING

I worked as a maintenance fitter for one of the largest bakery producers in the country and part of the job description was tracing pipework within the factory to make sure that pesky legionnaires disease wasn't lurking in dead ends of pipework. In the process of one of our redundant pipe searches we discovered that the pipe work that returned spent steam after heating the vats of cake ingredients had been inadvertently piped into the line of the cake-topping mix. Exactly how many years this water, treated with a variety of chemicals, had been pouring into cheerfully coloured cake-icings and fudges, I don't know.

I'm just glad I don't have a sweet tooth.

C. EDLEY

76 HOLIDAY CAMP CLEANER

Hours:
40hrs per week
Wages:
£1.33 per hour
plus lodgings

DISGUSTING

It was 1988 and I was eighteen years old. I was young, free and single and looking for a good time. An older sister of mine had done something similar a number of years before and had enjoyed it so I thought I'd give it a go, feeling sure I would meet some like-minded people, and that I could spend my summer working and drinking with others of my ilk.

Along with twenty or so other new recruits I got off the coach at the camp and we were shown to our staff chalets. These 'chalets', which we had to share with someone else, were tiny and shoddy in the extreme, consisting of two single beds, a wardrobe, a chest of drawers and a sink.

The toilets were in a block, so it was not uncommon for people to relieve themselves in the sink and I knew somebody who kept half a pool cue by his bed in case he needed a dump. He'd use the cue to poke it down the plug hole!

However, the 'chalets', known to employees as sheds, were at least free, as was the staff canteen. I need not tell you, then, that the food served up in this place would have made a dog puke. We got paid about £53.00 a week for 40 hours' work. And as for my fellow staff, as I've said, I expected to meet people like me - young, laid-back, carefree, etc. What I found were people who were on the run for one reason or another. Some were actually on the run from the police, some from debt collectors. Some people had come to work there to escape paying child maintenance, and others just to get over a failed relationship/marriage. In short what I found was the West Country's equivalent of the French Foreign Legion.

BRENDAN O'MALLEY

POO-DE-POO

41

75 SALMON HEAD SLICER

Hours:
9am-5pm
Wages:
£4.10 per hour

DISGUSTING, DANGEROUS

One of the worst jobs I've ever had was working in a fish factory, or more precisely, standing next to an industrial-sized bucket full of festering salmon heads for around eight hours a day. The job itself wasn't too bad, it was just the array of social outcasts and deranged ex-filleters I had to work with. There wouldn't be a day that passed without some joker's hands being thrust into the fish cake mincer, thus ensuring a fair amount of pure pork with the assorted eyeballs, gills and phlegm that constitutes modern mass-produced fish products.

The factory foreman looked and acted like a cross between the SAS's Eddy Stone and Jack Palance on angel dust, as he proceeded to terrorize just about anyone within the factory and a fair few innocent bystanders who just happened to be walking past. The general smell was one of a bloated whale's buttocks, and most of the females bore more than a passing resemblance to Charles Bronson (complete with tash and handgun). Due to the arctic conditions, I still get chilblains on frosty mornings, and yes, smoked salmon's definitely off the fucking menu.

SEAN BUTTS

74 MANAGEMENT CONSULTANT

Hours:
8am-midnight
Wages:
£20k + bonuses,
plus £10k golden
handcuffs bonus,
payable back if
you leave within
two years

SOUL-DESTROYING,
IMMORAL

Three and a half years ago I joined a well-known firm of management consultants, thinking I was about to enter an exciting career involving international travel and decent wages. Hmm.

Expecting glamour on my first day, I was sent to a business park in Maidenhead. The commute was two hours. The day I arrived the client had just sacked 2,000 people on our advice, so we were not popular. I realized that the reality of the job was working in an office where no one likes you and where you're just another faceless person in a sea of faceless people.

THE GLAMOUR,
THE FUN

Staff at the firm boast about the long hours they have worked. One girl boasted to me the other day that she had worked from 8am to 3am.

One of the absurdities of the job is the phrase, 'added value'. This meaningless bit of management bollocks is trotted out like a mantra. It has something to do with giving the client a good service, but is used as an excuse to force you into hours and hours of unpaid overtime, while you sit staring at a screen, crying, trying to 'add value' and trying to understand what 'add value' means in the first place.

The people who stay on and become managers give their whole lives to the company. My manager joked that he hadn't seen his wife for three weeks due to work. Two days later, his wife left him and he had a breakdown. He devoted one day to the breakdown and to his marriage, during which time he was constantly on the phone to us, before flying back to the Zurich office.

The culture is brutal. One day it all caught up with me; I'd been working so hard I started crying. The man next to me, instead of talking to me, sent me an email asking whether I might like to cry outside the office rather than in it. He graciously allowed me fifteen minutes off to compose myself. He assumed it was some personal problem and didn't realize that it was because I was so tired due to overwork.

The people who work at these places are rugby-playing twats of the highest order. They have no interest in books, art or music. All they are interested in is running the marathon. It's hell and I've quit. **ANON**

73 DAMAGED FOOD DISCOUNTER

Hours:
2pm-8pm
Wages:
£4.50 per hour

DISGUSTING, IMMORAL

I applied for a job in a supermarket. After completing a four-page application form I was invited to attend a group interview. Held within an airtight room during one of the hottest days in August, myself and four other would-be employees sat in strict silence wondering just what we were doing there. With thirst and the threat of asphyxiation growing steadily, we were forced to listen to a sixty-minute talk on the history of the supermarket and its policies on Health and Safety.

After a separate interview, we were shown another video about the supermarket's strategy, and were given a spelling and maths test. I was then offered a very promising position within a section called 'Data Management'.

My first task was to stand in the warehouse with an electronic gun and mark down by a few pence six containers of damaged goods. Leaking bottles of squash were Sellotaped up and marked down by 5p, split packets of crisps were patched up and marked down and this continued for six hours. I saw no daylight on my first day and was only allowed a twenty minute break.

LOST IN THE SUPERMARKET

On the second day I stood in the warehouse marking down by a few pence more damaged goods. Split cans of beans and dripping tins of tomato sauce were inspected by the supervisor and then begrudgingly thrown away. Open packets of pungent cup-a-soups were resealed and discounted while spoilt cans of tuna were bundled together and sold with a 10-pence reduction! Six hours later I left the warehouse, pale and stinking of various foods.

On my third day I marked down by a few pence four containers of damaged goods discovered during the previous day's trading. I again spent the day, minus daylight, standing around for six hours, being coated with various smells.

My fourth day in 'Data Management' saw me lazing around on a nearby beach, with my uniform and security card dumped the night before, on the street outside the supermarket in question. After three days of patching up dirty and disgusting products for cheap profit, and with zero help or support from my 'superiors', to say nothing of the dire work conditions and being lied to about the nature of the job in the first place, I took the decision to piss all over the dumped uniform as a form of protest - maybe the poor bastard who eventually took over my position got the chance to sell that at discount too.   **PAUL MILLARD**

72 INTERNET SUPPORT ADVISOR

Hours:
11am-8pm
Wages:
£9 per hour

SOUL-DESTROYING,
IMMORAL

I spent three months working in a large computer company's call centre. I was on the internet desk. Talking people through their first connection wasn't so bad, realizing that they had somehow deleted their connection and needed to be talked through the first connection procedure for the tenth time put a new angle on it. I quickly learnt that some people had the ability to accidentally screw up their machines many times. We did nine-hour shifts with one hour for lunch and two out of four shifts involved unsocial hours. We didn't start getting paid until we had logged on the phone. As such it was easy to lose an hour's pay because a queue at the drinks machine made you log on a minute or so late. We were not allowed to leave our desks for any reason (I ended up getting sacked for refusing to stick my hand up to go to the loo).

One of the final straws for me was the ruling about which calls should go through the £1.50 premium-rate line because having advised someone they had to call this line, it was likely that it would be me that answered their call anyway. One day I had a disabled man who could hardly speak or hear on the phone. It took him half an hour to talk me through his problem, describing all his basic details, and even though the maximum call length was ten minutes, I was still obliged to tell him to call the premium-rate line. If I hadn't been sacked later that day - only an hour away from completing my probation and thus receiving a pay rise - I would have resigned. **DAVINA GREGSON**

CRAP JOB TRIVIA

Falcon Cash and Carry in Leicester were forced to pay out £5,000 compensation to one of their workers in May 2004. The employee, a man with learning difficulties, had been paid 29p per hour for his first month's work. After this initial period his salary had increased to £1.04 per hour. The minimum wage in Britain for anyone over the age of twenty-two is £4.50.

71 PILL FLICKER

Hours:
8am-4pm
Wages:
£3.75 per hour

SOUL-DESTROYING

For one day only I flicked out-of-shape pills from a conveyor belt into a pile of similarly mis-shapen tablets on behalf of a pharmaceutical company. Mind you, by the end, I was letting some square ones slip through and flicking some perfectly round ones into the pile. It finally ended when I swallowed a large collection of both badly shaped and perfectly shaped pills.

ANON

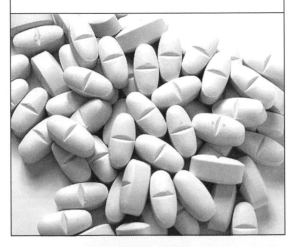

70 COMPLAINT-LINE OPERATOR

Hours:
10am-8pm
Wages:
£6.50 per hour

SOUL-DESTROYING,
IMMORAL

Everyone knows that call centres are crap – the sweatshops of the 20th century, modern slave trade, etc, etc - but my call centre job was really, really crap. After losing a perfectly reasonable office job I found myself lacking funds for an upcoming holiday and so decided that the best thing to do was to get a quick, easy job where I would have no trouble working extra hours for more money and which I could leave without any problems. So I walked into the nearest agency office and, a few days later, found myself sitting at a 'pod' (a cluster of four or five desks arranged in a circle), a pair of headphones on my ears, staring at a cheap computer screen that froze consistently and taking calls

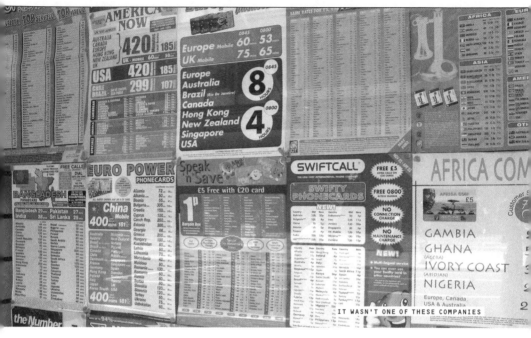

IT WASN'T ONE OF THESE COMPANIES

for a cheap phone-call card company.

Basically, people would buy cheap phone cards that would enable them to call relatives in far-off lands for half the price that BT offered. There was only one problem: the company and the service was complete and utter shit. The lines wouldn't work, the cards would break, the numbers on the cards were inaccurate the list goes on. This meant that the service only worked reasonably well for a few hours on a Friday afternoon.

For the rest of the entire week I took endless abusive calls from people who couldn't speak English. Often they would put relatives on to translate and I would find myself speaking to a twelve-year-old girl about the

FACTORY RULES, 1823 vs CALL CENTRE RULES, 2004

180 years of progress in the workplace

CRAP JOB TRIVIA

1823 Rules and fines of Tyldesley Mill, Lancashire	2004 Rules of a Call Centre, Sheffield
1) Any two spinners found together (talking): 2s fine.	1) Mobile phones must be switched off and out of sight at all times.
2) Any spinner being sick, and cannot find another spinner to give satisfaction must pay for steam each day: 6s fine.	2) If you want to change your shift it is your responsibility to find someone who is prepared to swap with you.
3) Any spinner found dirty at his work: 1s fine.	3) In order to maintain a clean, professional working environment, the consumption of food is not permitted.
4) Any spinner heard whistling: 1s fine.	4) Chewing gum is not allowed and we would ask that you place it in a bin at the start of your shift.
5) Any spinner leaving his oil-can out of place: 6d fine.	5) Please ensure that you tidy up any cups and rubbish from your desk at the end of every shift.

complexities of Telephone Line maintenance. Old women from India would begin to cry; men from Bangladesh would threaten me as they had nineteen and twenty-year-old grandsons living in London and they were going to come to the office, etc, etc. In the end the calls became so abusive, so endlessly bleak and nasty and difficult to resolve, that one day I walked in and decided not to answer a single call. You see I had worked out a little trick - when a call came through you simply answered it, put the caller immediately on hold/pause and left them there. They would think they were still in a queue and would continue to hold and not hang up; thus according to the computer and my line manager (an aggressive little man-hating lesbian, if ever there was one) I had answered and was dealing with the call.

I would pretend to speak to a silent line and then, loudly and politely, resolve the problem. My trick soon spread around my 'pod' and then the rest of the open-plan office. In the end I doubt a single call was being taken.

One day I was called in the manager's office along with my line manager and told that my attitude was wrong and that if I didn't 'pull my socks up' I would be fired. I couldn't believe that they weren't reprimanding me for what I had actually done and so I calmly stood up and said: 'This circus is over. So thank you and fuck you.'   **GARY COLES**

69 CHRISTIAN BOOK STACKER

Hours:
8am-5pm
Wages:
£4 per hour

HUMILIATING, SOUL-DESTROYING, IMMORAL, FUTILE

It was my great misfortune to be employed by a company of religious zealots. Before I go on I should point out that I was desperate when I took the job, which involved stacking boxes in a warehouse with these lunatics.

This 'Christian' organization, whose mission was to 'spread the word' through Christian book distribution, retail and publishing, had a policy of trying to employ people who were fundamental Bible junkies.

This policy was unsustainable,

as there were not enough wild-eyed crazies in the town. In no time at all at least fifty per cent of the staff were just normal Joes and Joesses and the biblical correctness of the management quickly went out the window as soon as staff shortages looked likely. These poor unfortunates had to endure a thrice-weekly and excruciatingly embarrassing 'devotions' period. These 15-30 minute episodes of happy-clappy mania occurred in the morning at 8.15am. Everyone was compelled to attend and paid to do so. It was part of the employment contract to put up with such ham-fisted attempts at indoctrination.

For Monday devotions there were departmental get-togeth-ers. It was here that keen-as-mustard juiced-in-the-ethos losers bleated about their God experiences. These were usually utterly mundane diatribes where some tosser thought about his nana's love when getting his breakfast and then proceeded

RACHEL POULTON

to bore everyone when he arrived at work ten minutes later proclaiming this revelation had the mark of the Lord. There would then be a closing prayer, again led by some holier-than-thou brown-noser. This creep would ask the Lord to ensure that the computers worked through the day, or that the boiler repairman coming to visit his home would have success in his fixing endeavours and other such tosh. I still recall clearly the drawn, glazed faces of the normal employees who had to withstand this garbage and the barely concealed glee of the happy-clappys as they watched our misery. Friday was a general assembly for all. Each week a member of the senior management 'led devotions'. These arse-lickers extraordinaire would stand and say all the right things as the CEO and his deputy listened. Other members of the management would eye us lesser ones,

checking our adulation levels. What they mostly saw was a sea of expressionless frosti-ness except for the odd beam-ing fundamental loony. Then came the prayers, which included more 'bless the office equipment' bollocks.

The working day at this hell lasted from 8am to 5pm and they paid well below the mini-mum wage. None of the brainwashed suckers com-plained though. One of them told me, 'We're not here for the money, we're here for the Lord.'

ANON

68 SEMI-CONDUCTOR PLANT GOPHER

Hours:
7am-7pm
Wages:
£5 per hour

IMMORAL,
DANGEROUS

My dad got me and my brother jobs once at the semi-conductor plant where he worked. We were gophers, carrying boxes of semi-conductor

wafers between the various processing plants in the build-ings as they underwent all the different processes.

My brother took the night shift, on account of the higher wages, and I took the days, on account of wanting a life. The twelve hour shifts were spent carrying boxes weighing 2kg each around in supermarket shopping

baskets (two boxes per basket) or occasionally, blissfully, pushing them around on a flat-bed trolley. Doesn't sound too bad, does it? Well, if you've ever worked in a semi-conductor plant you'll know that the successful production of wafers relies entirely on cleanliness. Wafers are extremely fragile and, when finished, can cost as much as £1,000 each. A speck of dust will render a wafer completely useless.

This meant that we all had to wear a 'clean suit', a large plastic baby grow with nylon and rubber boots, rubber surgical gloves, a nylon elasticated hood, a surgical mask and large plastic goggles. Pushing your mask below your nose to breathe when in the labs was a disciplinary offence. It was hot, it was August and there was no air conditioning, as that too carries dust. We had three breaks in twelve hours, totalling one and a quarter hours. At the end of each day I would arrive home at 8pm with only enough time and energy to bathe (as I smelt of sweaty potatoes), eat and crawl into bed ready to be up at 5.30am for work at 7am. For weeks after I finished working there my hair was lank, my nails soft and my skin sallow.

The company later became an enemy of my family when they almost poisoned my dad with a chemical that burns you from the inside out. They then made him redundant, although he was their longest ever worker (twenty-two years) and stripped him of his share options through a legal loophole.   **JUSTINE MARIE DAVIDGE, LLB**

67 GARDENER

Hours:
7.30am-5pm
Wages:
£3.50 per hour

FUTILE, DANGEROUS

I once spent an epic two months painting the white lines on school tracks and playing fields in the hills south of Croydon. For £3.50 an hour I pushed a trolley full of sloshing whitewash round and round and round these tracks, from 07.30 until 17.00, in sun and rain (which would wash all my hard work away before I could complete a single lap).

The white-line painting was far less eventful than the grass-cutting that I started on but got thrown off, luckily, before I got maimed. The Grass Master, a backward-looking bloke called Dave with straggly blond hair wasping round his ruddy blunt features, was an idiot. He invariably blamed me whenever his knackered lawn-mowers wouldn't start, even when I pointed out faults like empty fuel-tanks or missing spark-plugs. That helped break up the day, not much, but then the mind-numbing routine made the hours and days blur so I was always pleasantly and genuinely surprised to find myself on the bus going home.

I did make one lawnmowing friend and we had good laughs, even when he nearly killed me with his petrol mower. He let go of it while cutting a ridiculously steep embankment that led down to a chest-high wall and pavement that I was de-weeding. I heard his shouts and the approaching mower, fortunately I was crouched down anyway and just looked up in time to see the bouncing mower's blades swirl dizzily over my head, with snips of grass cascading down as it sailed past. (This scene was repeated years later in the helicopter scene in *The Matrix*.) Dave couldn't understand why I didn't find this funny.

Somewhat predictably, I actually 'lost' my mate through another accident. My mower smashed over a semi-buried bottle on a pavement verge and the broken blade and shrapnel zipped out and slit off the sides of two of his fingers. The noise from the mower drowned out his screams and I only realized what had happened when I saw he'd left his leaf-blower on the pavement, covered in blood, as he staggered off to find Dave to get driven to hospital. Dave told him to get the bus, that was the last we saw of him. Dave later spent ten minutes calling me a 'cunt' and a 'fucking cunt' for breaking his mower and losing another temp, while I just looked at him, baffled by his idiocy. My only consolation was that later that day Dave crashed his tractor-mower over a tree-stump and the blade ricocheted off a tree and cut his head open. Next day I was on white-line painting again and nine brain-dead weeks later I had accrued enough money to escape.
ROBIN TUDGE

SHELF HATRED

66 NEWSAGENT CASHIER

Hours:
9pm-7am
Wages:
£7 per hour

SOUL-DESTROYING,
DANGEROUS

Doing nights as a student at a 24-hour newsagent is undoubtedly the most miserable job I've ever had. People from the local nightclub would run in and kick the mop bucket over, or drag the front floor mat out on to the pavement to skin up on at 3 in the morning. The police would wander over occasionally if you phoned up hysterically enough, but the teenage criminals would wander away just fast enough to evade arrest.

This kind of work could turn you to drink, and in my case it did. Not content to drown my sorrows after work I took to stealing bottles of Diamond White from the shop and consumed them at work. I knew they were on to me as they often stock-checked, but they couldn't nail me because I never

57

got caught going home with any and there were never any empties in the bins in the shop (they checked). What I used to do was lift up one of the square ceiling panels that were within reach at the top of the staircase and lob the bottle in when I'd necked it. I threw so many up there that eventually, no matter which direction I threw a bottle, it would invariably make a loud clinking sound as it hit an old one. Well, all good things have to come to an end, and one day the deputy manager caught me pissed as a fart, giggling in a corner and stuffing a purloined egg and cress sandwich in to my face.

I was sent home, and at a later date officially sacked by the shop manager, who was actually a really good guy. He was all right about it, just a little curious as to where all the empties went. I never told him.

A few months later I found out that he had run away with £8,000 from the safe. As I said, he was a good guy. **ROB ALLAN**

Ye Olde Crappe Job:
COTTON MILL WORKER, 1845

From Engels' *The Condition of the Working Class in England*, 1845

The supervision of machinery, the joining of broken threads, is no activity which claims the operative's thinking powers, yet it is of a sort which prevents him from occupying his mind with other things. We have seen, too, that this work affords the muscles no opportunity for physical activity. Thus it is, properly speaking, not work, but tedium, the most deadening, wearing process conceivable. The operative is condemned to let his physical and mental powers decay in this utter monotony, it is his mission to be bored every day and all day long from his eighth year.

65 KENNEL WORKER

Hours:
8.45am-5pm
Wages:
£4.25 per hour

DISGUSTING

In an ingenious ploy to avoid the most distasteful elements of kennel work I adopted the posture of an animal hater, and was rewarded with a job in customer 'services' in the kennel shop. I cheerfully set to work lugging sacks of animal food from the warehouse, boxes of tripe and other doggy delights from the walk-in freezers, safe in the knowledge that other poor fools - who had felt a need to display their credentials as animal lovers - were 'rewarded' by the management with jobs such as shovelling dung.

But, as anyone cursed with the necessity of work can testify, the wheel of employment turns inexorably towards degradation, and so it was for me. One day I wandered into work, turning up my personal stereo in order to avoid the din of 100 deserted pooches, when I was informed that 'the boss' wanted to see me.

The problem, it transpired, was this. A few days before, someone had left open a door to one of the freezers containing frozen dog meat destined, in all likelihood, for a burger joint somewhere in the vicinity of Bracknell. The sun had, it turned out, also been shining on the now uncomfortably warm, nascent happy burgers, which had attracted the undivided attention of a surprising large local blow-fly community. The result of this happy union was discovered by the boss early that morning: maggots, thousands upon thousands of maggots.

My mission, whether I chose to accept it or not, was to remove the maggots, the rotten meat and then thoroughly clean the freezer. It was without doubt the most uncomfortable and distasteful two days of my life and as I set to work clearing out the maggots with my shovel I cursed the world of work and all the people who had placed me in this invidious predicament.

JAMIE

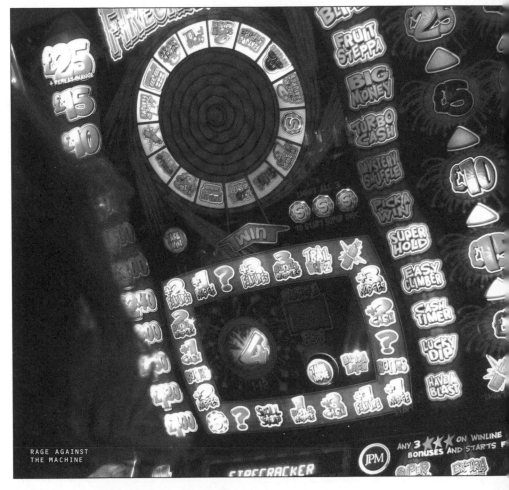

RAGE AGAINST
THE MACHINE

64 FRUIT MACHINE ENGINEER

Hours:
8.30am-5.30pm
Wages:
£8 per hour

DISGUSTING,
DANGEROUS

The job consisted of me driving from pub to pub in Coventry repairing fruit machines, pay phones and pool tables.

This must sound pretty good, spending all day in pubs, betting shops and amusement arcades, but it was not. It was hell. The average working day was spent in some of the most despicable dives, horrible urine-scented community pubs situated in the middle of desperate council estates, populated by whores, alcoholics and tattooed knuckle-draggers who used me to supplement their dole money by making false claims against the fruit machines so they could perpetuate their useless existences.

Aside from finding used condoms and syringe needles in pool tables, cleaning vomit off pay phones and the constant threat of having a pool cue wrapped around the back of your head for the sake of a handful of loose change, one of the worst aspects of the job was going into bingo clubs to repair their machines.

Bingo clubs contain some of the worst examples of humanity you would never hope to meet, bitter and twisted purple-haired harridans who believe they have a licence to treat you like shit because they were stupid enough to lose a week's pension money or their child's inheritance in a fruit machine. They would scream, shout and sometimes physically abuse you before going back to feverishly feeding pound coins into the machines with their withered, nicotine-stained fingers.

The slack-jawed no-hopers who staffed these places could never be relied upon to help you as they were always told to side with the customer, however ludicrous they were. Needless to say, I formed a very low opinion of the human race while working in that job, one that has stayed with me to this day.

ROGER EASTAFF

63 CHANNEL FIVE RE-TUNER

Hours:
10am-6pm
Wages:
£3.50 per hour

DISGUSTING

It was 'Mandy' – a woman with the complexion of an under-cooked oven chip – from a Croydon temping agency who suggested I go for the Channel Five re-tuning training course in Epsom. The course, which ran for three mornings, would enable me to 're-tune' TVs door-to-door.

It all seemed simple enough during training and after watching the videos depicting various dos and don'ts of conduct I set about my job.

One notably bad experience among many others occurred when I called upon a man dressed in nought but a soiled vest and underpants. He obviously hadn't had any visitors for some considerable time, but after insisting that I tune in the TV immediately, he reclined on his sofa, and covered his modesty with his crap-encrusted duvet. The vast and exclusive collection of anal buggery videos openly displayed on his shelves should have given me a clue that he was quite a lonely chap. I had to test the video signal so I hesitantly placed one of these into the video and fumbled about with the TV whilst trying to not look at the screen. Suddeny I heard a faint yet ominous rustling behind me. Ignoring this, I continued, fearful of what I might discover. I eventually turned to find him cracking one off over his duvet, apparently deeply stimulated by the reality of human company. I didn't hang around, but simply fled, ashen-faced and disturbed, into the streets of Enfield.

WILL HOGAN

62 ADVERTISING SALESMAN

Hours:
9am-5pm
Wages:
Commission

SOUL-DESTROYING, IMMORAL

A friend of mine had recently started work at a media sales company and was making lots of money fleecing marketing directors by selling space in a famous news agency's yearbook - a great-looking glossy mag of the sort you find in aeroplanes. Its content was a bit dull, probably even by the standards of the people it was intended for, and full of stock photographs and news items from the financial world. On every other page was an advert for some luxury car/holiday destination/blue-chip company, etc, etc. This magazine was a 'spank' in sales speak - an easy sell due to its patronage.

I didn't get to work on it, though, because I was placed in the charge of a boss I shall call DJ, and I was to work on a magazine about golf. I had no interest in golf, so it didn't bode well. DJ was likeable enough to start with, all pep talks and forced matey-ness, but I noticed that something was not quite

GWYN

right. He was constantly on edge for some reason. Looking around the office, I quickly saw the kind of people that media sales attracts: people who need to make money fast. It was full of coke-fiends, abrasive ex-public school wankers with halitosis and other assorted ne'er-do-wells who would get their £2,000 in cash on Monday but still demand a sub on Thursday because they'd blown it all on their opulent lifestyles. DJ was no exception. He was invariably late, pasty of face, shaky, messy of hair, chain-smoking and surreptitiously swigging something from a medicine bottle. Once he had calmed down, he would get down to some work, which involved him muttering into the phone to one of his definite leads. Sometimes he would come away from the conversation stressed, other times it would be all high fives and 'bad-a-bings'. I had no such luck. I had to generate my own leads from the stack of magazines in the office. They were all either crap or someone else's lead (and you must never, ever steal someone else's lead). I hated talking on the phone to twatty CEOs, etc, who had heard the script (or one of its many variations) before and were not interested in the magazine. DJ would be on my case if I wasn't on the phone, and when I was he would sometimes interrupt me during my pitch and try to get me to parrot him - this I found extremely confusing, and that irked him somewhat.

There were a lot of dodgy deals going on, freebies instead of payment, and I accidentally let slip about one of DJ's to my friend on the yearbook. DJ was fuming. He stood glaring in the office doorway and beckoned me with his index finger. I endured a tirade of abuse, but he quickly backed down when he realized the trouble I could get him into.

I was a success, of sorts, eventually. I got a musical instrument maker on board (as they'd say), and a luxury hi-fi maker was interested, but wanted to trade equipment for the ad-space. I was unable to say yes to this but, needless to say, DJ's ears pricked up at the promise of a freebie. He wanted it so bad that he offered me £100 for the lead (and my silence). About a week later he took me out into the stairwell to discuss my future with the company (another tirade of abuse). This time I was not prepared to take any shit, and stood smirking at him as he lost his temper. He offered me an ultimatum, and I said I would leave. His face dropped. I had him by the balls - I knew enough to get him sacked. As I walked down the stairs, he came running after me in a bit of a panic. 'I still owe you the money, everything we've discussed is between you and me, OK?' He rang me a few weeks later, when the mag was published. My name was on the sales team for his shitty golfing mag.

JOHN FERGUSON

61 PIPE COUNTERWEIGHT

Hours:
8am-5pm
Wages:
£5 per hour

😑^zz
FUTILE

I was once employed to stand on a pipe for two days. A building agency sent me to work as a labourer for some pipe fitters two floors underground in the dingiest cellar known to mankind. My task was to counterweight the pipe while it was set level by standing on it.

Why the hell they couldn't just have found a lump of stone to do my job (thus saving themselves £90) beats me. It is a sad state of affairs when you realize that a lump of stone could actually do your job better than you.

GIDEON BERRIDGE

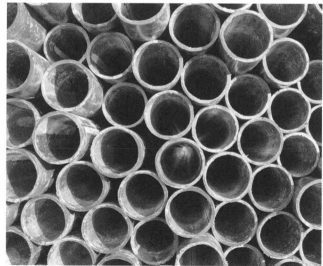

60 NIGHT OFFICE CLEANER

Hours:
10pm-6am
Wages:
£4 per hour

HUMILIATING,
SOUL-DESTROYING

The thing that gave this crap job its icing of crapness was the 'people' I had to share this hell with.

Firstly, there was my boss, a crazed old blue rinse bat aged about eighty who spent the time chain-smoking L&B in the foyer, moaning about the police 'victimizing' her family and friends and finding ways to avoid signing off my payslips. Then there was my 'supervisor' and her seventeen-year-old daughter who alternated between chaining L&B, poking at her belly-button piercing, which had gone very septic, and finding the worst jobs possible in the building and giving them to me. Making up

the rank-and-file was the boss's fourteen year-old son, who never did a stroke of work but just smoked and played on a Gameboy all night. This left all the actual work to be done by me and a big guy called Tim.

Tim was tattooed all over and had several teeth missing (he'd lost them in a fight after he hit someone with a pool cue in a nearby pub) and even the inbred management seemed scared of him. He also had strange ideas about how best to lighten the workload – rather than use the Hoover, he explained, he found it easier to

THE GREY GRAFTERS

New socio-economic category to describe oldies for whom retirement is a distant dream. Example: Tony Shelley, 78, who toils as a supermarket butcher. In a recent piece of pro-work propaganda in the *Sun* newspaper, he describes his punishing schedule: 'I am up at 3.30am and leave the house at 4.30am to get there by 5am. I then have a cup of tea and get ready to start work at 6am - then I'm on till 11.30am.' In return for donating so much of his time to a company, Tony gets £6.14 an hour, or £135 a week after tax.

CRAP JOB TRIVIA

LOST IN A
SPIRITUAL VACUUM

scurry about on all fours, picking up the bits of fluff and crap by hand. I suggested that I'd use the Hoover. He looked down at me menacingly. I spent two weeks scurrying about on all fours looking for carpet lint.

Finally, as well as having to spend eight hours a night with a bunch of losers lording it over me with the power that came with their 'supervisor' name-tags and one semi-deranged gorilla, I had the added fun of contending with the sleep-deprived, underpaid and justifiably cranky nocturnal employees of the office, who liked to moan about the shitty standard of cleaning we were providing at every chance whilst they lay about waiting for a telecommunications crisis to justify their existence. On my last night a guy who looked like he'd swallowed a KFC outlet whole, and who was attempting to smoke through the air-conditioning vent at the time, complained that my half-hearted 4am dusting was giving him asthma, and that I ought to get some GCSEs and a proper job. I became a seething ball of pent-up rage and left within the half-hour. **TOM ROYAL**

59 PEA CHECKER

Hours:
4am-12pm
Wages:
£5.10 per hour

HUMILIATING,
DISGUSTING

This job entailed literally watching conveyor belts full of peas and looking out for black ones. When you stand up you feel as though everything around you is moving, even though it's not. And you get a hole in your visual field for green, so everything looks redder than it was after an eight-hour shift. Miserable.
JEREMY IRELAND

Ye Olde Crappe Job: SEWER FLUSHER, 1849

From a letter to Henry Mayhew

We pulled up an old sewer that had been down upwards of 100 years, and under this there had formerly been a burying-ground. There we dug up, I should think, one day about seven skulls; and tremendous lot of leg-bones, to be sure! I don't think men has got such leg-bones now. The stench was dreadful. After that bout I was ill at home for a week.

58 CHILLI SAUCE BOTTLER

Hours:
8am-7pm
Wages:
£4.20 per hour

FUTILE

After a five-minute monologue extolling my own virtues, the woman in the recruitment agency smiled politely and asked, 'Have you got any industrial work boots?'

Two days later I found myself in a warehouse in the middle of an industrial estate somewhere in Welham Green. Said company imported various foodstuffs from the West Indies - most of the site was given over to warehouse space, with dizzyingly high towers of coconut milk cans on pallets. However, one side of the warehouse had been converted into a bottling plant for what was undoubtedly the most unpleasant substance they dealt with - West Indian hot chilli sauce. This stuff made depleted reactor waste look like baby moisturizer: you entered the factory through a series of hermetically sealed rubber flaps and almost instantly your throat tried to jump out of your neck, due to the searing fumes that filled the single-room 'plant'. As if this wasn't bad enough, there was the work itself.

The chilli sauce came in huge blue plastic barrels, into which a hose was jammed.

A rather Heath-Robinson looking machine sucked the gloop out of the barrel and filled up bottles that ran along a conveyor belt. My job was to take bottles off a palette and put them on the conveyor belt. The only other person in the room was the poor sod who had to stick labels on the bottles as they came off the machine at the other end. If the label was not perfectly straight, the psychotic supervisor (a slightly fat little woman, who can't have been over 4ft tall) screamed bloody murder at my unfortunate co-worker (liberally infusing her invective with 'bloody students'). To make matters worse, after about two hours of exciting bottle-moving fun, the supervisor came in and said, 'Oh, you seem to have got the hang of it' - and then proceeded to turn the machine on to 'light speed' setting. Oh, and we weren't allowed to talk, in case it distracted us. It got worse on the second week.

TOM WHALLEY

57 BROADCAST EXECUTIVE

Hours:
9am-6pm
Wages:
£14.50 per hour

HUMILIATING, FUTILE,
SOUL-DESTROYING, IMMORAL

Also referred to as TV Planner or TV Executive this job entails buying 'airtime' (or slots/spots) from TV stations where your clients' ads will appear. So a big client, say BT, might spend £10m on a single campaign and it is your job to ensure it's spent wisely (i.e. in a targeted and cost-efficient manner) across 100s of channels and 1000s of programmes. The job is twenty per cent hard-arsed negotiator, eighty per cent data-inputting gimp. The bulk of your time is spent booking thousands of these spots on to archaic computer systems.

As with most jobs in the media you soon discover that you are in fact doing your boss's work for him. This is fine as long as you accept the unwritten guidelines, i.e., that when it's good your boss will take the credit and when it's bad you'll get a right kicking.

The clients treat you like scum and moan about how their ads were only in crap programmes. Auditors get to say your work is shit and the Media Planner who looks across all the media mix gets to put you down too.

But the worst thing about the job was trying to explain what it was I actually did for a living. I tried repeatedly to explain to my mum but to no avail. How do you explain to someone of that generation that buying blank space between crap programmes is a profession?

So after my eighteen months it was back to the dole for me - I felt it was more honest that playing a tiny part in selling people crap they don't need. I can't say there was any physical hardship to the job but as we know it's the mental scars that take longest to heal.

TARQUIL HAVERSHAM

I WENT TO UNIVERSITY FOR THIS?

56 INDUSTRIAL BAKER

Hours:
7am-4pm
Wages:
£4.50 per hour

SOUL-DESTROYING

I once spent a month standing beside a conveyor belt placing little plastic dishes on its constantly moving surface. I then spent another month (having been promoted) placing pieces of factory-fresh apple pie in the constantly moving dishes that had just been placed there by the new guy standing next to me. I then spent another month (yes, I was promoted again) fitting little plastic lids on to the dishes of apple pie after the most experienced guy had pumped a dollop of custard on to each piece with a giant custard machine.

These delightful pastry products were destined for a number of well-known airlines. The industrial bakery took itself very seriously, developing new products and producing everything to a uniform crap-airline-food quality. After three months I was beginning to seriously doubt my sanity.

Then one Monday morning I was summoned to the manager's office. Uh, oh, I thought, maybe they have found out about the bag of defective croissants I liberated from the store room as a present for my mum. When I walked into the manager's office I was greeted by the sight of three senior members of the management team standing in a row behind the desk. The section manager who got to have a blue band on his white baker's hat was there. (We wore white wellies, disposable boiler suits and hair nets and hats?) So was the factory floor manager with his red hat band and, most impressively of all, the factory manager with, bizarrely, his brown hat band.

I was shown to a seat and the factory manger ceremoniously cleared his throat and began. 'It has come to my attention,' he said, nodding towards the section manger, 'that you have done an excellent job.' In other words I had stayed longer than three months in their bakers' hell. 'So we have decided' - nod of his brown hat to the red-hatted boss - 'that' - dramatic pause - 'we are going to put you in charge of the custard machine!' They all beamed at me and awaited my response. A voice inside my head screamed: 'I've got to get out of here!'

And so I did just one week later. But the really scary thing is that by the time I left I was directing the filling of the enormous custard machine with some pride, reprimanding the new guy for filling it with 7 litres of custard instead of 7.5 litres as regulations required, and double-checking the thing had been cleaned properly before I left each day.   **ANON**

55 BATTERY BREAKER

Hours:
8am-6pm
Wages:
£1.20 per hour

SOUL-DESTROYING, DANGEROUS

Back in 1983, I answered an advert to be a storeman in a battery warehouse. When I started, I realized what we really did. We were to spend all day, every day, breaking batteries to retrieve the lead cores.

These were batteries from trains, and weighed about a hundredweight each. You'd drain the acid into a trough, slam the battery at an angle to break the pitch seal, and then the lead core would fly out.

You then had to put the lead core on to one pallet, put the plastic casing on another pallet, grab a battery off another pallet, and get going again.

This was the mind-numbing routine, broken only by two fifteen minute breaks and an

hour lunch.

Your protective gear was a boiler suit, rubber apron, goggles, wellies and long rubber gloves. Now, to pick up something that heavy, you need to hold it close to your chest. The acid always found a way in. Everybody got burns on them. I got them on my belly, legs and ball-bag, as well as the odd splash in the eyes.

STEPHEN MURRAY

54 SPERM TESTER

Hours:
9am-6pm
Wages:
£8 per hour

DISGUSTING

On any given day, I perform approximately four hundred tests on samples taken from various patients, for many different reasons or diagnosis. Apart from the miserable stool culture, the examination that I hate the most is the dreaded 'Semen Analysis'.

Excuse the pun, but just conceiving where it came from gives me the willies. The paperwork usually arrives before the specimen, giving me the name of the person whose semen I am about to get close to. I always imagine a middle-aged man in the bathroom just down the hall, or maybe in his car, doing his level best to conquer and defeat his male organ and obtain that climactic juice. The worst part of the whole scenario is seeing whose 'sample' it is as they hand over their 'job-well-done jar' to the receptionist. Then I can match a face to the name I already have.

So then, after all the men's intense toiling and exertions to 'acquire' the semen, I subject it to all forms of cruel testing procedures. I attempt to measure the sample and then spend a good couple of seconds 'sucking' the specimen up a pipette and expelling it numerous times back into its container. The only problem with this part of the testing is that frequently while I am 'playing' with the specimen, a slight whiff of the substance reaches my senses, and I am then forced to fight back the dreaded gag reflex. A few more of those actions and it's then time to squeeze the semen specimen back in the jar and cap it tightly before something unfortunate happens.

According to Carl, the cleaner, his job is much worse than mine. Apparently not all the semen makes it into the jar and he has to wash down the chairs and the carpet after men with no aim have occupied the cubicles. Maybe that's where they've been going wrong.

HEATHER WERNETTE

53 SILO CLEANER

Hours:
6am-6pm
Wages:
£2.25 per hour

DISGUSTING,
DANGEROUS

Starting on a dairy farm in September after a particularly warm and lazy summer, the farmer informed me he was having trouble emptying his slurry silo. The once liquid contents had become increasingly solid over the summer months and lost their ability to flow. The sticky brown stuff occupied the bottom 12 inches of the silo - itself about the size of a tennis court - and, having added another 12 inches of water overnight, my job was to climb in with a spade and mix the two parts to a more fluid state. This took the best part of two days in blazing sunshine - after which the bastard still would not empty and we had to repeat the process with another 12 inches of water. Having completed the task, I climbed down the metal ladder and accidentally trod on an electric fence, electrocuting myself in the process. **PHILIP CLARKE**

SILO, SILO,
IT'S OFF TO
WORK WE GO

52 SOCIAL SECURITY CLERK

Hours:
8am-5.30pm
Wages:
£7 per hour

DISGUSTING, SOUL-DESTROYING

After a year of temping I applied for a job at a Job Centre. After two weeks of staring out of windows and at pretty students (it was summer, a lot of students sign on in the summer) I was deemed fully qualified to advise people on their careers. How hard could it be? I had to be better than the old bag and the shallow-breathing alcoholic who'd dealt with me when I signed on. The first thing you realize is that sane people, nice people and generally people with a sense of humour don't sign on for very long. Class A drug-addled schizophrenics, greasy-haired stereotypical computer gimps and social inadequates still living off the glory gained at school from bullying the fat lad

do however sign on for a very long time... at least that's how it seems.

Every now and again I'd have to swap the chair in front of my desk for another one because I knew the stain was piss. Every now and again I'd throw all my biros in the bin because the green-skinned man on methadone put one in his mouth and then put it back in my pot and all biros look the same. Every now and again I'd listen to the old grey-haired Marjorie Dawes clones I worked alongside moaning about 'muslims' ('I'd never let a kid of mine grow up to be a suicide bomber').

The fact that I had to smile sweetly as I told people, 'No you can't have any money, yes I know you've paid taxes for thirty years, and I know the lad next to you hasn't paid any because he's a drug addict and a thief and you're not, yes, I know your wife has just died and that's why you'll have to spend your life's savings in order to survive.' That was bad enough but the main problem was that I just didn't want to be there. Life is just too short for crap jobs.

ALLEN SIMON

AND THIS LITTLE PIGGY WAS
LIQUEFIED, SYRINGED AND
THROWN INTO A CAN

51 HAM FACTORY WORKER

Hours:
8am-6pm
Wages:
£4.10 per hour

DISGUSTING

Ever wondered how ham is made? Well you take the bits of pig that are not actually used as meat (feet, lips, skin...) and empty them into a big wheelie bin, this is then dropped into a giant blender to make a sort of liquid pig mixture. This stuff is then cured and poured into a big stainless-steel syringe thing. Finally you get a temp to hold long steel tins up to the end of the syringe and fill it up with liquid pig, then throw it into an oven.

This might not sound that bad, but until you've been hit in the face with cold pig's blood and spent an evening trying to get solidified pig fat out of your hair, you don't know you've lived.

That said, you could get cheap frankfurters on a Thursday, so it wasn't technically hell.

PAUL CAMILLERI

50 COACH DRIVER

Hours:
7.30am-4.30pm
Wages:
£8 per hour

DISGUSTING, SOUL-DESTROYING, DANGEROUS

The worst job ever has to be coach driving in the UK. It's not just the horrendous traffic and brainless HGV drivers putting everyone else at risk by driving with a mobile phone glued to their ear whilst eating a meal and watching their portable telly two feet behind some poor sod in a Skoda. No, it's the passengers themselves that are the real pain. From foul-mouthed schoolkids, who treat your vehicle like a playground, leaving food and chewing gum plastered all over the coach, and who call you all the names under the sun when told to sit for their own safety, to urine-smelling pensioners who moan about everything, even when they are on a free trip paid for by social services. Then you have the late-teen to early-thirties nightclub set. Oh, what a joy they are, vomiting, pissing and defecating in the coach that you just spent three hours getting spotlessly clean. If you have the temerity to complain, you usually end up in hospital being stitched back together, such is the mentality of clubbers. Then you have the holiday makers. They arrive with portable wardrobes instead of 'one medium-sized suitcase' and look astonished when you tell them its over the weight and size allowance. They are told when they book that the coach is non-smoking yet moan loudly about it, asking why we can't stop every half-hour so they can light up, whilst the non-smokers grumble that we stop too frequently. When arriving at the destination, the coach driver gets blamed for the lousy hotel/bad food/bad weather and the fact that some stupid woman lost all her holiday money on the first night by feeding it into the fruit machines at the nearest amusement arcade. Worst of all is having forty-nine back-seat drivers! I finished up putting a sign on the back of my driving seat: 'Would all passengers who think they can drive this coach better than me please take note of the mistletoe on my shirt tail!' **G. K. RYLAND**

49 CINEMA POPCORN SELLER

Hours:
4am-12pm
Wages:
£3.20 per hour

 DISGUSTING

The worst job I ever had was working for a cinema in Nottingham. The uniform was regulation prison issue, polyester trousers with a stripe down each leg, a snazzy waistcoat and a button-on bow tie. They had a tiny room with no ventilation or natural light, where I would make (literally) tons of popcorn (sweet and savoury) using a huge brute of a machine that would spit hot popcorn out at you periodically. At the start of the job I would gorge myself on popcorn and then proceed to feel ill for the entire eight-hour shift. At the end of the day cleaning the greased-up monster of a machine was exhausting. I would then re-enter the real world, blinking and rubbing my eyes, as they grew accustomed to natural daylight again.

CONOR WHITWORTH

SICKEST JOBS

This list shows which job types pull the most sickies per year. We would suggest that in general, the more sick days taken, the worse the job. The national average is 7.2 sick days per year.

Sources: Home Office, CBI, Welsh Audit, National Audit Office

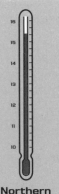

Northern Ireland Civil Service: 15.4 days

Welsh NHS staff: 15 days

Prison Officers: 14.7 days

Teachers: 13 days

Police Officers: 11.55 days

48 SCHOOL ADMIN ASSISTANT

Hours:
8.30am-4.30pm
Wages:
£4.75 per hour

 SOUL-DESTROYING

I had a job in the reprographics department of a secondary school. It was a disaster from the start. Queues of teachers psychotic with stress screamed for their copying to be done immediately. It was impossible to keep up with these 'emergencies', let alone the work they left in the tray for, 'when you get a moment'. I never got a moment.

I came to see the cramped little room I worked in as one big amplifier, which was sensitive to my every move. If I hit a wrong button on the copier (forgot to select 'enlarge A4-A3' for instance) it wasn't just one mistake, but 240 mistakes, or however many copies were run off. The book keeping was similarly frustrating, all done by hand, written in columns so that an incorrect number in the middle meant that all the figures which came after it were wrong and had to be laboriously erased with correction fluid and re-entered. Thomas De Quincey had an epiphany in St Paul's Cathedral Whispering Gallery when he realized that the multitude of echoes emanating from a single point were like decisions taken in the present, which then grow

YOU CAN TAKE YOUR PHOTOCOPIER AND STUFF IT RIGHT UP YOUR ARSE

and become the tangled, intractable situations of the future. His eureka moment became my Hades. Those papers flying out of the copiers were the reverb echoes in some kind of nightmarish King Tubby or Keith Hudson track. A single pulse of information duplicated times X, which became a metaphor for determinism. Doing things right first time was the key, but as I was constantly under siege from all angles it was impossible not to make mistakes, molehill-sized mistakes which grew into Mount Everests of wrongness and had to be addressed. I asked the school manager to dismiss me after three months. I can no longer listen to the dub records I once loved dearly.

STEVE HANSON

47 CALL CENTRE OPERATOR: MEDICAL INSURANCE

Hours:
8am-6pm
Wages:
£4.25 per hour

SOUL-DESTROYING,
IMMORAL

Telesales is low. Stuck in a retro (in other words, hopelessly outdated), sweaty office with other desperate bastards, all attempting to 'sell' private medical insurance, it was my task to sit at a phone line and recite the script. Not make phone calls, because the wonderful computer dialling system would do that for me, resulting in a ring tone appearing as soon as the last 'customer' had told me to piss off.

The product of this was five to six hundred phone calls a day, for the most minimum of minimum wages, and a bonus, which would be received if we hit a target of twelve. That's twelve successful calls out of 600, a target few of us ever hit.

Ever called a dead man's wife trying to sell her private medical insurance? Or the sister of a mentally challenged child? Or spent the traumatic hours of 9–11 calling people to sell them accidental death cover? I shit you not, it happened, most of it on a daily basis. For the record, no insurance company will cover these people - surprising that - and they, in all their spluttering rage, know it.

I received three death threats during this period of my life, and one bonus. That being the day I told my boss I couldn't make one more call without going postal, and walked. **K. GRIFFITHS**

TELE SALES TEMPS NEEDED

MUST HAVE 1.YEARS OF BUSINESS TO BUSINESS SALES EXPERIENCE

DONT MISS OUT CALL IN TODAY

46 PIE HOLEMAKER

Hours:
7am–2pm
Wages:
£3.50 per hour

DISGUSTING,
SOUL-DESTROYING

Have you ever bought a pie from a supermarket? Yes? Then you may have noticed that the pastry lid has a small hole in it, which allows the vile contents of the pie to release steam while cooking in the oven.

You would have thought this was a prime candidate for mechanization, but no. For a few weeks, those holes were made by yours truly, as I tried to earn some cash before beginning a degree at university. What a way to start your working life.

Ten-hour night shifts were spent standing by a conveyor belt with a metal spike in my hand. The pies came past at a rate of one every 43 seconds, which meant I could watch them slowly approaching before adding the final touch. Add to this endless torture a clayhead bint working next to me who insisted on talking loudly about her active sex life, and you can see why the pleasures of the job were limited.

If you've ever bought a supermarket pie that looks like it's been vandalized that was me, taking out my frustration on the innocent consumers. No, I'm not sorry.

MARKUS EICHHORN

45 CHARITY COLLECTOR

Hours:
10am-6pm
Wages:
One third of takings

IMMORAL

You might not have realized that charity money-box rattler is actually a job in the paid sense of the word. But I was paid a third of the takings for standing round supermarket entrances, rattle-box in hand, and wearing a big sash with the charity's name emblazoned on it. God knows what the charity actually did. I got this job through the Job Centre and naively assumed that it must therefore be some kind of respectable post.

Anyway, the charity shop front was just that, a normal store of flakey games and books and old clothes, but through the door at the back was a more complex operation. In a long fluorescent room were three desks, two of which were for counting the proceeds of the rattlers and the third commanded by a fat 'gore blimey' bloke who had a briefcase full of used notes (really, he did) and two TVs, one on Channel Four racing and the other on Ceefax Racing all day long. Whenever I returned from whichever site he'd dispatched me to the day before, he'd be there, counting notes and shouting horse-odds to someone even further out the back. He was affable enough and gave top tips for getting good

takings. My third cut of all those pennies, free of any tax or NI contributions, was incentive enough. But neither he nor the others there ever explained properly what the charity did or what their remit was, which meant I could only fudge my answers to inquisitive pension-ers parting with their pennies 'for the children'. And it really was the case that the poor were the most generous.

ROBIN TUDGE

44 DIRECT DEBIT ACTIVATOR

Hours: 9am-5pm
Wages: £5 per hour

 FUTILE

Hundreds of little grey slips came to my desk every single day, and it was the mental equivalent of a conveyor belt at a factory. The same repetitive task over and over again. But the ancient computer system was slower than you could (theoretically) work, expectations were low and quality control even lower. So to cope I just stopped working. There were enough other people doing the same thing to cover my idleness.

Paid by the hour, I came in late and went straight for a mid-morning nap on the (empty) top floor. After a two-hour lunch at the pub or smoking joints in the park it was time for mid-afternoon football in the empty canteen with another temp. Then it was home time. Each week my timesheet was signed by someone who worked at a different office so I could easily say I had worked forty hours. One afternoon I came back from lunch so drunk on vodka I passed out at my desk for three hours. No one noticed. I lasted nine months and if they looked in my drawer afterwards they would've found 5,000 inactivated direct debit slips. **SIMON LUKER**

Ye Olde Crappe Job: MATCHMAKER, 1863

From *Mr White's Report on the Lucifer Match Manufacturer in King's Cross*

A wretched place, there being at one end an open hearth with a fire burning. At the nearest end of the chief workshop, a long and fairly lighted but ill ventilated room, a man was preparing the materials for the composition; at the other end was the dipping slab. Between these are ranged the children at their benches. Beyond this is a room a few feet square, with a hatch opening on to the dipping slab, and also having lucifer matches stored in it, and beyond this again... the drying room, close and hot from the stove where the mixture is heated. Nevertheless in this small room between the workshop and drying room close by the hatch, a boy and girl fill frames.

In this drying room the late owner, Mrs Halsey's husband, was burned to death a short time since in trying to put out a fire, said to have been caused by a child out of mischief...

43 LABORATORY ASSISTANT

Hours:
8.30-5.30pm
Wages:
£8 per hour

DISGUSTING

I worked for a large pregnancy testing firm as a lab assistant, the dosh was OK and I thought lab work equals warm, easy and clean. How wrong can you be! The firm were making a scientific rhythm method product (contradiction in terms but...) based on the standard pregnancy test sticks you can get. As a kind introduction I was lead to a huge walk-in fridge by a grey geezer who proceeded to entertain me with some excellent anecdotes of his (long) time working for Huntingdon Life Sciences. A good start, I thought! The fridge was packed with a tumbledown mountain of several thousand semi-frozen sample pots filled with women's piss. The job was to sort out the samples into cycles, so after a day rummaging through leaking frozen piss pots and getting soaked in frozen stinking stale piss whilst being hassled by various anonymous grey techies, I

thought what the hell, go home, get shitfaced and go in again to see if it was going to be more of the same. If it was, I could always walk. Poverty is an excellent motivator.

So roll on day two. I woke with an evil hangover and proceeded to the lab. I didn't think anything could be as bad as day one but I was wrong. I was tasked with exposure-testing these piss sticks, and ended up standing in front of a garden-sprayer filled with gallons of urine. I had to clamp these sticks into a frame then spray piss on to the sticks. This was not great fun, especially as they had been using the piss for several months and it smelt like nothing on earth. There were even some amorphous jellyfish-like creatures floating in it! The best bits were doing miss-tests, which as you can imagine generated some excellent spray. Another day covered in stinking piss... I didn't make day three.
ANON

GWYN

88

42 PLASTIC TRAY CHECKER

Hours:
9pm-9am
Wages:
£2.50 per hour

FUTILE,
SOUL-DESTROYING

The factory was based in Chorley, Lancs, and made plastic containers and other plastic products. I had the job working nights (with my brother and a few mates) checking plastic food trays for minute imperfections (holes, cracks, etc). All night long we squinted at trays together, working under a bright lamp. To say we felt like lab rats would be an understatement. We each had ten pallets waiting to be checked.

After three hours, we gave up. It was a twelve hour night shift but to finish the shift would've been a living hell. We all walked out together with a permanent squint in one eye and left behind the princely sum of £2.50 an hour. Bastards...   **IAN LEACH**

41 MILK PROCESSOR

Hours:
6am-5pm
Wages:
£5 per hour

DISGUSTING,
DANGEROUS

Ah, buxom, rosy-cheeked milk-maids carrying wooden pails... Ermintrude-like cows with flowers in their mouths... yuh, right.

The milk comes out of a pipe, into waxed cardboard boxes, which become the familiar tetra-paks. Tetrapaks are fitted into trays of a dozen, which are then shrink-wrapped. When the trays come out of the wrapping machine, they're hot as hell, and guess who has to pick them up. Oh, yes.

They then get placed on vast pallets. There's a specific pattern. There's a precise gap between each pallet. On the first layer, the trays go north-south, the next layer they go east-west. Sterilized milk goes on blue pallets, full-cream on brown. Twenty-four trays on each pallet, stack them six high and wrap with another layer of plastic. Unfortunately, nobody bothers to tell me this, so when the supervisor comes round after an hour and a half of wasted effort, I get a profound bollocking for slamming them down any old how. This, apparently, is very amusing, according to my colleague, the mad-eyed fork-lift driver. Another worker joins in with the laughter, then, when the driver leaves, informs me that his colleague is the only worker not in the local rugby team, because he's 'a queero' and 'will shag any hole there is'. Did I mention we were in Devon?

I get the hang of the process, and the work gets... well, not 'better', but maybe marginally less vile. Then we get a 'burster'. A carton is slightly overfilled, and the pressure of the heat wrapping causes its warm contents to erupt over my face. It's like an industrial bukkake video.

I become a vegan.

TIM FOOTMAN

NINE TO SKIVE
According to a DTI Survey in 2002, twice as many UK workers would rather work shorter hours than win the National Lottery.

40 CORNISH PASTY FACTORY WORKER

Hours:
8pm-7am
Wages:
£7.90 per hour

HUMILIATING, DISGUSTING

(———) pasties
(———) pasties
You can chew and chew and chew
They are tasteless through and through...

By far the most crap job I have ever had was working the night shift on the crimping and packing lines of a cornish pasty factory in Cornwall. It was the summer before I moved to London and I desperately needed to save money before leaving home. Working from 8pm until 7am, donning a little hair net and uniform, I was often in tears before the nightmare shift began.

Those damn machines were fast and relentless, the endless racks of metal trays holding a constant stream of pasties, pies, sausage rolls, slices, Scotch eggs and other meaty products of unknown substance was nothing to the horror I felt upon meeting my fellow employees. All were pale and pasty, some were inbred, none had ventured out of the five-mile-square radius that comprised their world, one had a mangled hand and all were sexually frustrated.

There was no life outside of the factory, only the dark throbbing womb of the pasty and pie production line. And those who could drive never ventured beyond the safe confines of the A388 - a road that took them from factory to home and back again!

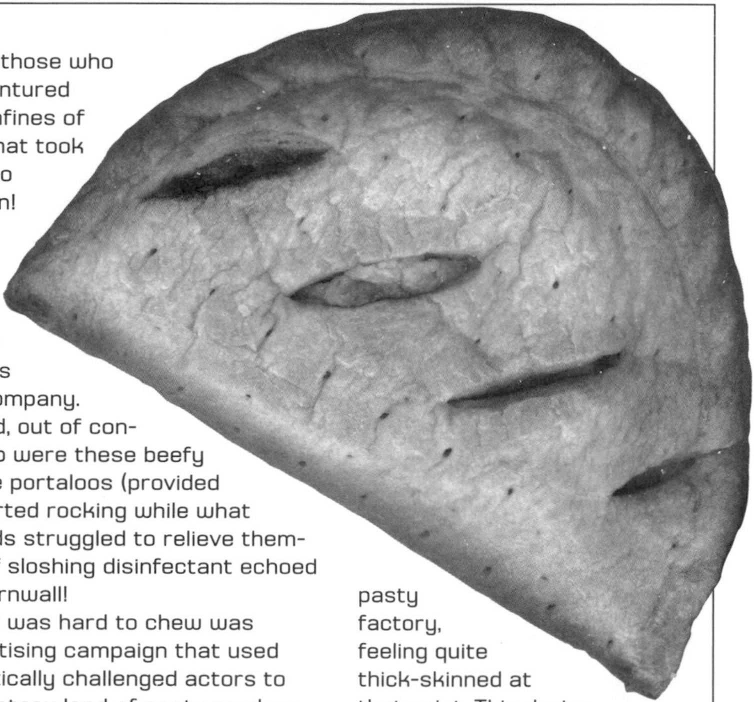

One memory still gives me night-mares. It was a staff do of sorts, a treat for the shack-led employees of this vastly successful company.

The staff went wild, out of con-trol, and so sexed up were these beefy pie stuffers that the portaloos (provided for the evening) started rocking while what seemed like hundreds struggled to relieve them-selves. The sound of sloshing disinfectant echoed round the hills of Cornwall!

Another crust that was hard to chew was witnessing an advertising campaign that used dwarfs/midgets/vertically challenged actors to portray a surreal fantasy land of pasty produc-tion. This was quickly taken off the air after numerous complaints. The irony was that it was-n't so far from the truth.

When arriving in London on my first day at col-lege we had to introduce ourselves and inform the new class about what we had done over the summer. I was brave and bared all about the

pasty factory, feeling quite thick-skinned at that point. This daring act prompted the girl next to me to admit that she was in charge of stuffing the strings into tampons in a tampon factory.

ANON

91

'AFTER FINISHING WORK EVERYTHING
SMELT OF URINE, MY BODY, FOOD,
GIRLFRIEND, MOTHER'

39 HOSPITAL LAUNDERETTE ATTENDANT

Hours:
10am-8pm
Wages:
£6.15 per hour

DISGUSTING

The launderette was a hot, loud cathedral-sized warehouse filled with gigantic tumble driers, massive washing machines, and very strange people, all dedicated to cleaning the bedding, surgical gowns, nappies and towels of the entire hospital. Masses of dirty laundry would come down these big shoots. They would be covered in shit, piss, blood, and once, with what looked like someone's kidneys. As the new employee, I was put on 'dirties'. This meant I had to stand under the shoots, catch the laundry, and transfer it into a washing machine. I spent most of the day with my face in or near piss. After finishing work, my nostrils were impregnated with the stench of urine. Everything smelt of urine: my body, food, girlfriend, mother. It took three weeks after quitting before I could smell anything properly again.

But like all crap jobs, there was an upside: the pleasure in some-one else having to do it once you'd moved on. I was shifted, promoted if you will, to machine operator, after I had persuaded a similarly down-on-his-luck friend to join the launderette. As the new employee he was now on 'dirties'. My new job was to press a button when my machine made a funny noise. It was a great job, but made me even more idle when I started sitting on the floor and using a broom handle to press the but-ton. Such initiative didn't go unnoticed, and I was moved on to bigger machines with more buttons, some of which flashed.

But the eventual departure of my friend left a vacuum on 'dirt-ies'. I was fucked if I was going to go back to tasting piss, so I walked. **RALPH EL TURK**

93

38 COLD-STORE ASSISTANT

Hours:
6pm-9pm
Wages:
£8 per hour

HUMILIATING,
SOUL-DESTROYING

Based in east-London premises resembling sinister medical blocks, the Cold-store invited two dozen saddos per night to ponce about on motorized pallet trucks picking orders from the 'pots' (fridges) to load on to articulated lorries for delivery to supermarkets.

'If it says peas on the order form, you pick peas,' said Dean, the supervisor. 'If it says fish fingers, you pick fish fingers,' he added, displaying the intellectual acumen that, no doubt, would one day result in his Nobel Prize.

The colleague detailed to supervise my first 'pick' was Norman, a bloke very well versed in frozen foods and, suspiciously I thought, Under-15 girls' wrestling. Norman knew the quickest ways from Ice Creams & Sundries to Ready Meals via Fish Products, but I had the feeling things were becoming a trifle steamy under his frosted protective suit, especially when describing the technical intricacies of the Half Nelson.

After three hours of numbing cold and non-stop perversion I was ready for a cup of tea in the canteen. But Dean was waiting for me. 'Fucking goujons!' he roared.

'You what?'

'The list says fucking fish fingers and you've put fucking goujons on your pallet, you tosser!' This was obviously a big deal. 'Don't you even know the fucking difference between fish fingers and fucking goujons?'

'Yeah, but Norman was doing the list,' I protested, looking around in vain for my instructor. 'Where's he gone?'

'He's in the khazi, mate,' sniggered one of the blokes already drinking tea.

'He always goes to the khazi for his break.'

'I wonder why,' I asked, chucking my gauntlets on to the table. 'Oh well, Dean... goujons to you, you thick twat.'

This effort at intra-personal workplace relations was...well, goujons, and I fled before Dean got more than four of his brain cells working simultaneously and thumped me. I have never returned to the Frozen World. **MIKE COLLINS**

37 DOMESTIC-SECURITY SALESMAN

Hours:
8.30am-1pm
Wages:
Nil

IMMORAL,
DANGEROUS

As with many others, my initiation into the world of work was not a pleasant one.

My sorry tale begins with a desperate search in the *Nottingham Evening Post*. It yielded few results until my gullible eye drifted down to one of the boxes promising 'Part Time Hours with Full Time Wages'. Never one to turn down an easy life I gave them a ring - and was invited in for an interview that very same afternoon. WOW! I thought. I must have impressed them!

That afternoon, wearing my best, and only, Grattans suit (which I was still paying for every week) I joined a bunch of other 'hopefuls' for an aptitude test to see if I was suitable for a

career in domestic security system sales. After filling in one side of A4 with a well-chewed bic biro, the results were collated. How my pride swelled at being informed that I was an outstanding candidate, scoring in the top 5% of the general public! The fact that all twenty of that day's group got through the test was, I was assured, unprecedented.

The next morning I turned up at 9am for 'training', which consisted of a ninety-minute presentation by the company's top salesman (an ex-SAS sergeant called 'Wes'). Basically we had to knock on doors all over the city and get people to sign up to free security checks on their home. For each check we signed up we would get £5, after which a 'security specialist' would attend and explain what problems there were with the security, and perhaps suggest a solution from the company itself. If they sold a system I was in line for £50! Wes's methods of securing a 'sale' just relied on not taking no for an answer and not leaving the doorstep at any point - even if the door was closed in his bulldog-like face.

It didn't take long before the task of knocking on doors suggesting they let a total stranger come round to look at the locks in their home dragged a bit....after knocking on about forty doors in Long Eaton I hadn't yet secured one booking. However, my disappointment was eased by the fact that I had also not received a black eye from the less than hospitable individuals on the council estate I'd been sent to. Not only did I have to move swiftly to avoid Rottweilers and gangs of youths hell bent on stealing my clipboard, but I was also constantly hounded by Wes, who was driving around after us all in his black BMW M3 telling us to 'get sales or else'.

At lunchtime we were ushered back to Wes's car for a 'team chat'. Basically, he flew off the handle and warned that anyone who failed to get at least two sign-ups in the afternoon would be in for 'a severe beating' come 5pm (or 'zero hour' as he referred to it). He then offered us some white 'Marching Powder' from a little wrap to 'make us focus'... an offer I declined.

I spent the rest of the afternoon in a pub on the estate spending the last of my dole money on pints whilst trying not to make eye contact with anyone in the place as I was sure my suit made me look like CID. **PAUL VINTER**

36 FREELANCE MAGAZINE DESIGNER

Hours:
10am-6pm
Wages:
£13.50 per hour

HUMILIATING

On my first day as a designer for a men's style magazine, the art director decided to illustrate a piece using lots of women's faces at the point of ecstatic orgasm. 'As an initiation' I was sent to steal images from obscure, foreign hard-core porn mags. Everyone took great pleasure in sending me round Soho to buy all the copies of *Barely Legal* I could find. Then all the men in the office (about 95% of the staff) stood around laughing while I blushingly cut out the women's faces.

LIZ HARRIS

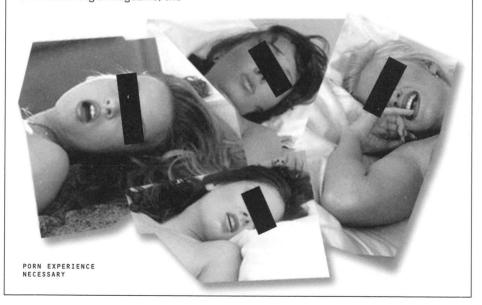

PORN EXPERIENCE
NECESSARY

35 CHEESE FACTORY HAND

Hours:
8am-6pm
Wages:
£3 per hour

 DISGUSTING

After an unpleasant incident with my bank manager in the summer of 1996 I was reluctantly forced to get a job through a temp agency.

As I lived in a remote Cheshire village and had no transport, the only option was to work in a cheese factory. I did this for three months and every time I think about it now I have to hold back tears of pain and regret.

My job involved working in the packing room for £3 an hour. Huge heavy blocks of stinky cheese sweltering in the humid factory heat would trundle along a conveyor belt. One of the deranged cheese packers would slap it into a tin box and

CHEESED OFF

stick it in a compressor where it had all the sweet-smelling cheese juice squeezed out.

When it was ready, the box would be passed down to me. I had to grab it, slam it down and wrestle the cheese out, chucking it into the store room. I'd then bang the box apart and pass it to a fat middle-aged man who hated me because on my first day I put the parts through in the wrong order and fucked up his 'system'.

The boxes came thick and fast, all day, every day. If I stalled on a box they'd pile up and crash off the conveyor belt, causing the packing team to laugh hysterically. By the end of the first week my hands were in tatters, I'd lost half a stone due to the heat and constant toil and I stunk of rancid Cheshire.

The only relief was being sent to the scraping room. This represented cheese factory R 'n' R because it involved scraping bits of mould off huge slabs of cheese. The smell was indescribable. After a week, my co-worker, a middle-aged violent Teddy Boy confided in me that he occasionally liked to make holes in the blocks of cheese and have sexual relations with them. I asked for a transfer back to the packing room.

The high point of the job was watching a deranged Mancunian take a £5 bet to jump, fully clothed, into a huge vat of curd.

MATT BROWNSWORD

34 CEMENT RESEARCHER

Hours:
8am–5pm
Wages:
£7.40 per hour

SOUL-DESTROYING

Last summer on my university summer holiday, I worked at a nuclear reprocessing plant. Before I even arrived I had taken all manner of shit off righteous anti-nuclear arts students. I was a cynical engineering student who was bitter about having four 9 o'clock starts a week, and I had a vendetta against anyone with fewer lectures. Also I wasn't actually working with anything vaguely nuclear anyway. I was researching cement and was beginning to wonder how I was going to spend ten weeks miles from anywhere.

As part of the deal I was given free accommodation in a 'training and accommodation centre', i.e. an empty travel inn in the middle of nowhere. It had an empty bar that was only open Monday to Thursday, I began to feel as if I was living the life of Alan Partridge in the TV series. The only saving grace was a brilliant pub at the end of the road. It was our only contact with the outside world and we managed to spend £300 each over five weeks. It was basically a choice between becoming an alcoholic or going mad.

The work wasn't so bad, when there was some to do. Two weeks before I arrived all funding for the research team I was in had been stopped, so there was absolutely nothing to do. I spent the first four weeks on the intranet (no internet access) or hiding in a corner of the lab sleeping. It got to the point where when I was given Excel spreadsheets of corrosion data to work through (make a graph, delete any points that don't look right) I was actually excited. At least it was better than going back to the travel inn in the evenings. Needless to say I won't be going back again this year. **ANDREW DONOVAN**

33 DOOR-TO-DOOR SALESMAN

Hours:
9.30am-5.30pm
Wages:
Nil

HUMILIATING,
SOUL-DESTROYING

I sat in a small reception room with six sorry-looking souls when a tanned man with a golden mullet burst through a side door.

'HI!' He was American. 'My name's GARY! Who wants to make money? YEAH? YEAH!'

He came over and shook my hand rather too vigorously.

'We've got a great job for you here, Colin. You like to work hard?'

I muttered 'yes' like a drone.

'Well that's great! We're the best at making money here y'know! If ya go down to the front door Eddie's waitin' for ya!'

A moment later I was outside with eight young lads, all dressed in suits and all eagerly sucking on Lambert and Butlers and not talking. A guy who looked like he'd had a few too many speed-balls came over.

'I'm Eddie. C'mon.'

He set off walking at such a pace that I momentarily forgot that I still didn't know what the job was. We all got on a bus. The lads spoke about how they all made 'about 16K'.

Of course, it was door-to-door selling. Up and

down a bloody big hill in an old mining village. Eddie was going to show me how to sell deal leaflets for two local 'restaurants'. Things didn't look good at all.

Every house we visited seemed to be occupied by mad Nazi pit-bull breeders or crying, fourteen year-old mothers. We stopped at a pub for lunch and I saw a man eat a raw potato, while another sat laughing and pointing in a way that only the genuinely insane can.

My feet were bleeding but I persevered. I thought that once it got dark we'd head home. We didn't.

When we finally got back to the 'office', Gary was waiting for us. He counted in the cash from Eddie and the other 'marketing executives', kept some for himself and gave the rest back out before congratulating each of us. A perfect example of the whore/pimp nature of capitalism.

Then, without warning, a huge brass bell came out of his bag. He rang it so loud I nearly shat myself. Over this clanging he started to bellow:

'WHO'S THE BEST?'

'WE ARE!' everyone shouted back. Over and over. I left the room to spend the next four months on the dole recovering from the experience. **COLIN THORNE**

Ye Olde Crappe Job:
BEEF LARD FACTORY WORKER, CHICAGO,1905

From *The Jungle*, Upton Sinclair, 1905

The worst [jobs]... were the fertilizer-men, and those who worked in the cooking rooms. These people could not be shown to the visitor, for the odour of the fertilizer-man would scare any ordinary visitor at a hundred yards; and as for the other men, who worked in tank rooms full of steam, and in some of which there were open (boiling) vats near the level of the floor, their peculiar trouble was that they fell into the vats; and when they were fished out, there was never enough of them left to be worth exhibiting - sometimes they would be overlooked for days, till all but the bones of them had gone out to the world as Durham's Pure Leaf Lard!

IMAGE FROM *THE JUNGLE* BY UPTON SINCLAIR, PUBLISHED BY PENGUIN CLASSICS

32 JUNK MAIL COPY-WRITER

Hours:
9.30am-7pm
Wages:
£15 per hour

SOUL-DESTROYING,
FUTILE

Ten or so years ago, after a period of 'rest' following redundancy as a writer in advertising, my mortgage-lender eventually jollied me into finding a new job. I went to see a headhunter who sent me for an interview to a publishing house (who shall remain nameless but you'll know them as one of the biggest purveyors of 'junk mail' in the UK). They looked through my portfolio, and I was then showed some of their creations, and asked to comment on them. The words 'unbelievable rubbish' and 'instantly binnable' immediately sprang to mind, yet after three interviews with old crumbly people who smelt of stale coffee and old office carpets, I was surprised to be offered a freelance position as a senior writer instantly

- and at a vastly inflated sum per week.

I turned up on my first day, knots in my stomach, expecting to be found out and dismissed - only to discover that my boring, monotonous life was about to begin. I was left with a prissy, prematurely aged spinster who told me that I could start on The Envelopes. And my brain-busting task? To change an N to an M, or a 3 to a 5. Over and over and over again, creating a new Word document with header each time in a creaky old computer system.

The horror of it all was that you were expected to do hundreds - I mean hundreds - of these meaningless documents a day. At first you think, I need the money, I can hack this. Then you start making mistakes because your brain goes to sleep - or worse, in my case, you rebel against The System by trying to write something new - for which I was severely reprimanded.

QUEUEING UP FOR THE SLAVE TRAIN

I used to steam with frustration and boredom. Worse still, a host of weirdy gnome-like anally-retentive proof-readers would send back *all* my documents to do again because I'd sinned by using the wrong kind of hyphen, or the wrong size full-stop or some such mind-mashing soul-destroying nonsense. These people had no lives, so no one chatted or socialized. No one was married or had children. No one had any hobbies. Some of the bosses lived nocturnal lives, only emerging from their cave-like offices when it was quiet, to grub around for fags or cold coffee from the machine, or snuffle papers around and steal the freelancers' ideas to claim as their own. The genteel back-stabbing that went on was excruciating to watch.

Sadly I became institutionalized and didn't find the will to escape until nearly five years later. Please let me remain nameless. They might still try and claw me back in. ANON

31 DATA INPUTTER

Hours:
9am-6pm
Wages:
£5 per hour

SOUL-DESTROYING,
FUTILE

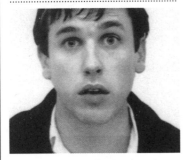

Four years ago I joined various high street temping agencies who didn't seem to mind that I had no idea how to work a computer and had never been near an office in my life.

They got me jobs stuffing envelopes and making coffee - perfect employment for an idle git like me. But soon I hit pay-dirt. MAFF (Ministry for Agriculture, Fisheries and Food) were looking for a general office monkey, or 'data inputter', for the Fisheries

Department for at least half a year. They were prepared to pay me the jaw-dropping sum of £5 per hour.

I snatched up the job and almost instantly wished I hadn't. If you ever get lucky enough to go inside MAFF you will notice that it is peopled by Papa Lazerou's circus freaks from *The League of Gentlemen*. I think they must have some sort of government quota on how many general accidents of nature they employ at any one time. In my office we had an army-mad lad with a lisp and a fat, sweaty, balding middle-aged wreck of a man who had clearly come straight to MAFF after leaving school in the sixties and had never plucked up the courage to leave. Every day he would come in half an hour after me, and flop into his chair with a sigh of soul-destroying sadness. He clearly hated his job, but got some kind of perverted gratification from sighing and tutting and carrying the weight of the world on his rounded and flabby shoulders.

All I did was file. Everything was copied in triplicate, stamped and then put into a paper file - usually covered in dust - and stored in rows. There must have been thousands of them. I suppose government ministries need to keep records, but this lot kept everything, no matter how trivial.

What's more, my colleagues clearly thrived on filing. They loved it. People often complain about bureaucratic people and red tape. Well, I've met the people who make this red tape and, I can assure you, they get a big kick out of it.

After three months I couldn't take any more. I was waking up every morning close to tears. It was destroying me, sucking the life from me. I started looking for an excuse to leave. Then one day I was asked to file a whole month's worth of correspondence on the import of Fish Gametes into the UK. It took all day. Like so many times before, I had no idea what I was working on and didn't really care much. However I decided to ask what a Gamete was.

'Sperm,' was the simple reply.

I digested this, and wondered why on earth we were importing tons of the stuff each day. I then started to worry about how the fish muck was harvested in the first place (now that really is a crap job!). So I asked why we wanted so much fish semen. 'To put in fish paste,' was the reply. I left the next day. **FINLAY COUTTS BRITTON**

30 HOSPITAL ADMINISTRATOR

Hours:
8.30am-5.30pm
Wages:
£7 per hour

SOUL-DESTROYING

I worked one summer in the administration section of a rehabilitation hospital. I had to visit the offices in the wards daily to update the in-patients' charts with any new results of blood tests, X-rays, etc. Most of the offices were located at the end of the ward, which meant that I had to walk past all the patients to get to the files.

This was absolutely fine, except in the High Dependency Unit.

There was one patient who had been in a particularly nasty car crash, and was made to sit up in his bed for two hours every day. If I made it to the ward before the bed was tilted, he would lie silently staring at the ceiling. However, if I was running late, I would get there while he was sitting, and I could hear him muttering something over and over under his breath.

After a few days of this, my curiosity got the better of me, and I walked deliberately slowly past his bed.

I remember the horror I felt when I suddenly realized that what he was saying, over and over, was 'Kill me. Kill me. Kill me...' **SHARON**

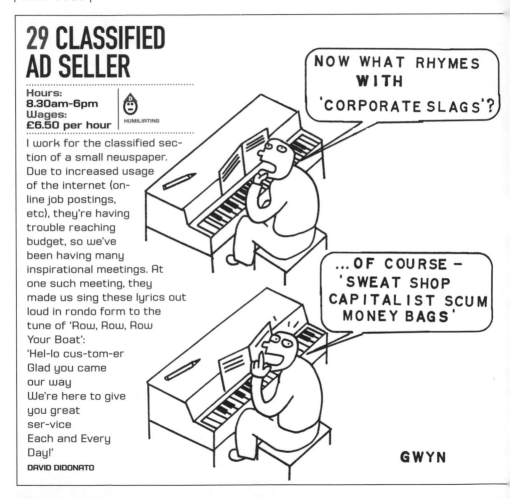

29 CLASSIFIED AD SELLER

Hours:
8.30am-6pm
Wages:
£6.50 per hour

HUMILIATING

I work for the classified section of a small newspaper. Due to increased usage of the internet (online job postings, etc), they're having trouble reaching budget, so we've been having many inspirational meetings. At one such meeting, they made us sing these lyrics out loud in rondo form to the tune of 'Row, Row, Row Your Boat':
'Hel-lo cus-tom-er
Glad you came
our way
We're here to give
you great
ser-vice
Each and Every
Day!'
DAVID DIDONATO

NOW WHAT RHYMES **WITH** 'CORPORATE SLAGS'?

...OF COURSE — 'SWEAT SHOP CAPITALIST SCUM MONEY BAGS'

GWYN

CORPORATE SONGS

In the old days, the powers that be made you sing hymns to nurture the work ethic. Nowadays, companies use rousing songs to encourage loyalty in their employees. Here are a few snatches from our favourites:

CRAP JOB TRIVIA

Sun Microsystems

The power of Sun, will blow you away!
Best range of product, on the market today!
A different game, has really begun
We make it happen – with the Power of Sun!

Texas Instruments

We're customer focused
And drive to succeed
Technology entitlement, you do it with speed
Commitment, integrity, you care, you wait
The pace is relentless, you must innovate

Ericsson Wap Rap

Have you seen the light yet, baby?
Seen the WAP glow in your neighbour's eyes?
Do you want to get wireless with me tonight, baby?
Give me your number, and I'll send you something you'll never forget

IBM

Ever onward! Ever onward!
We're bound for the top
To never fall,

Right here and now we thankfully
Pledge sincerest loyalty
To the corporation

UNISYS

We eat, sleep and drink this stuff
U-ni-sys!
We eat, sleep and drink this stuff
U-ni-sys!
We eat, sleep and drink this stuff
Oooh yeah, Unisys!

AT & T

(To the tune of 'We Are Family')
We're AT & T, one big happy family.
We're AT & T, all the Business Units and me.
We're AT & T, everything you want it to be.
We are family, the one and only AT & T.

KPMG

We're strong as can be
A team of power and energy
We go for the gold
Together we hold on to our vision of global strategy.

28 SANDWICH FILLER

Hours:
8.30am-6pm
Wages:
£6 per hour

DISGUSTING

I worked in a sandwich factory for a miserable pittance in the summer after my GCSEs. The permanent staff were bitter and resentful of my youth, so they made me do all the crap elements of sandwich-making – yes, there is a hierarchy to making sandwiches.

I was always in charge of the eggs, which were stored, pre-boiled, in vats of fluorescent yellow vile-smelling liquid. I had to rinse them, shove them through a giant mincing machine and then dowse them in several industrial-sized jars of cheap mayonnaise. This was especially unpleasant in the stifling heat, while suffering the full-effect of a never-before-experienced hangover. Being in charge of the buttering machine, in contrast, was a much-coveted job in the factory. The machine was both easy to use (you simply tip the sliced loaf into a chute, and it pops out at the other end ready buttered) and fun (you could really challenge yourself by attempting to achieve records in the buttered loaves per minute league, or you could go quite slowly and become transfixed by the gentle rhythm of the slices popping out of the machine).

But these 'pleasurable' jobs were scant and heavily outweighed by more mundane activities like scraping off great swathes of grated cheese

(cheap, warm and rubbery, of no fixed origin) from the preparation tables or mixing huge trays of stinky tuna mayonnaise.

There are two women from that time who will forever be lodged in my memory: Betty Gums and Betty Lettuce. Betty Gums had false teeth and peculiarly pale gums. She was a sweet, timid woman. Betty Lettuce always washed the lettuce. I don't know whether she chose to do this or was forced into it at an early age. She was a fiery woman, old before her time, whose daughter once tried to kill her. The other employees who stand out were a gay man who denied being gay and said his live-in lover was a flat mate, and a power-crazed chef who would stomp around on the floor above us, sporadically sending down pieces of cooked meat on the dumb waiter.

Happy days. **JESSIE SANDERS**

27 LANDFILL EXECUTIVE

Hours:
8.45am-4.45pm
Wages:
£3.15 per hour

DISGUSTING, HUMILIATING

I was once employed to cover eleven years' of Northamptonshire's rubbish with plastic bin liners. My instructions were simple. I was to meet a guy called Dave and he'd tell me what to do. First Dave laughed for quite a while about my clothes (T-shirt, shorts and trainers). Then he pointed me towards a haystack-sized roll of black bin liners on a metal cart, sent me out of the hut and told me to go round the corner and 'up the hill'.

I turned the corner and stopped dead in my tracks. As far as my eyes (which were filling with tears) could see was a mountain of black gunge. It stretched out far to the left and far to the right and for ever straight ahead. I walked up to the foot of the mountain and pressed my foot against it. It gave way and then sprang back to its original shape, which was the shape of nothing.

And it smelt of burning turds.

The gunge had decomposed to the extent that each bit of crap looked and felt exactly like every other bit of crap. I wheeled my trolley past plastic tubes conveniently placed at head height and expelling trapped methane. I found a group of men, all in white boiler suits and gas masks like you see on films dealing with aliens/small nuclear mishaps. They were pointing at me. The men probably saw the fear and nausea in my face as they didn't laugh at my inadequate clothing, and only looked at the ground and indicated that I was to start laying the bin bags over the gunge.

The idea was that when I had finished they could lay turf over it and little bunnies could live there. I estimated that this would take me the rest of my life to achieve. I factored in the remuneration (£3.15 per hour worked, no paid lunch break), dropped my cart handle on the floor and hurried home for a smoke. **PETE MCGAUGHRIN**

26 TEAM-BUILDING HELL

Hours:
A whole weekend
Wages:
Nil

HUMILIATING

One of my worst job experiences was when I had to take part in a team-building weekend. One evening, in the middle of a swamp in Florida, several hundred employees gathered for an evening of fun and games. In my taupe-coloured team T-shirt, I and nine other employees who I'd never laid eyes on before, joined together to compete against the yellow, orange, brown, rust and other putrid-coloured teams.

After a barbecue of fried alligator and bison burgers, the sun went down and the games began. First, I had to bounce on an oversized rubber ball with a limp triangle for a handle through a muddy path. Then there was the water balloon toss - in the dark. I don't think I caught even one, well, not with my hands anyway. Then I had to race with an egg in a spoon and a ping pong ball

balanced on a ping pong bat.

Next, we lined up, each with a foot-long length of hollowed-out pipe. Peas were then let loose at the front of the line and we were meant to join our pipes so that the peas made it safely to a bucket at the end of the line. With each pea that dropped, the team member at the end of the line ran to the front of the line to begin the whole thing again.

We had a number of peas in our bucket, but it was too dark to see for sure if we had seen more peas to safety than the orange team with whom we were competing. I had made it through an entire rotation and was at the end of the line when one of my team members turned to me and snapped: 'You're doing it wrong!'

At that point, I stood up straight, handed her my length of pipe and said: 'Will you excuse me? I've got to find the loo.'

I then walked out of the swamp and into the parking lot where I quickly found a bus back to my hotel room.   **RAQUEL BAETZ**

25 SEED PROCESSOR

Hours:
6am–2am (with breaks)
Wages:
£3 per hour

DISGUSTING,
SOUL-DESTROYING

Every summer whilst on holiday from university, my best friend and I used to put up marquees until it was harvest time, when we would both sign on as 'Seed Processors'.

This job involved travelling around to farms in a transit van with a diesel genera-tor in the back, following a lorry with a big machine on top that processed grain and sorted the more viable grains so they could be used as next year's seed.

Doesn't sound too bad, does it? However, it also involved standing next to this vibrating machine as lorry after lorry of grain was passed through it, coating the grain in mercury-based agro-chemicals and emptying the result into 50kg bags through a hopper that would fill at an alarming rate. It was a constant race against time. You kept going until the job was done, and the machine would not stop until it was all taken care of.

So on a shitty windswept farm in Lincolnshire, for example, you would be deafened by noise, wearing a cheap paper mask as you put bag after bag on this hopper, stitched it and then, when it was full, lifted it on to a lorry. And it was bloody heavy - about 50kgs - 8 stone. By the end of the job you were covered in shit, chemicals and dust. A typical 50-70 ton job would involve twenty bags per ton. 1000-1400 bags. Christ. We would work up to twenty hours per day and seven days a week (at £1 per ton!), then pack up and start driving to the next farm. You had to get used to sleeping in barns, vans, anywhere...

By the end of the season you would have muscles in places you shouldn't have and be totally unable to talk to anyone at all. The worst incident was bagging 70 tons in the driving rain and darkness under floodlights in Cumbria. There was a river of shit and silage passing through the stock yard at 20 miles per hour and six inches deep. Once, a cow that was being passed through the yard gate collapsed and the farmer sent for the vet. He arrived, shot it in the head at close range and then put a metal spike in the hole and wiggled it around to 'stir its brains up'.

The Horror.

TIM ROSER

'BY THE END OF THE JOB YOU WERE COVERED IN SHIT, CHEMICALS AND DUST'

24 COLD CALLER

Hours:
9am-5.30am
Wages:
Nil

HUMILIATING,
SOUL-DESTROYING, IMMORAL

After a string of bad temping gigs I came across an advert in the *Evening Standard* headed simply, 'Earn up to £100 a day.' I already had a pile of non-essential CDs lined up for the Record and Tape Exchange so I figured I had nothing to lose. I called the number and, with all the zeal and pride of the desperate jobseeker, described my many glorious achievements. It didn't take long. The voice at the other end of the phone was remarkably unforthcoming about exactly what it was that I'd have to do to earn up to £100 a day, but I was invited to an address in Zone 6 for 'training' the following Saturday.

So, three days later, I shelled out six quid for an all-zone travelcard and an hour later took my seat with a dozen others in a room, somewhere in Middlesex, that contained only chairs, tables and telephones. It smelt faintly of fish.

Confidently, I proved that not only could I speak English, but I could also count. I was then inducted into the talkative world of telesales. The company sold paper by the ream. 'Commission only, no private calls, no deviation from the script, no conferring, nothing allowed on the desk, one hour for lunch, start Monday.'

On each table was a dainty little parlour bell. When you made a sale you picked it up and rang it. It was kind of medieval.

To earn £100 a day, I now estimate, you'd have to be making a sale about every ten minutes. It took me fifteen minutes just to work through the script.

I did that job for a week - never deviating from the script - offering garage mechanics in Burnley free samples of shampoo with their reams of paper, persuading harried doctor's receptionists to switch supplier, asking grocers if they'd ever considered the advantages of switching to a heavier grade of foolscap... I didn't make a single sale.

The bells pealed around me as pustulent sixteen-year-olds read their scripts with a winning mix of menace and charm. By Wednesday the twelve of us who'd started had been reduced to seven, and by Friday I too was forced to admit defeat, crushed by the following brutal equation:

Outgoings: six travelcards, plus sundries £40. Earnings: nil.

JON FORTGANG

23 WEED SPRAYER

Hours:
7.30-7am
Wages:
£3.75 per hour

DISGUSTING,
HUMILIATING

One of the worst jobs I've ever had was one summer after I'd dropped out of university. I took a job as a weed sprayer. Every day I had to wear a green boiler suit, carry a bright yellow 35-litre tank of toxic weedkiller on my back and a sprayer in my hand. This look was finished off with lime green marigolds and a face mask. My twelve-hour shift consisted of scaling the banks that run alongside motorways, spraying around the little trees at the height of summer to prevent the poor things being overpowered by bramble and other violent plants. My chronic hayfever made an already hellish job much worse.

When the three months of this motorway

purgatory had ended I went on to spray the streets of Slough, which, comparatively speaking, I was looking forward to. But it proved to be much worse. At least on the motorway banks I was an anonymous fool, but now my humiliation was there for all to see. Imagine how you would react to the sight of me spraying your pavements.

Four-year-old children ran up shouting, 'Ghostbuster!', laughing in my face and calling me a twat, dickhead, etc. Capri drivers would honk their horns and yell 'sad bastard'. There was nothing I could say or do, no witty retort could hide the fact that they were right.

One day an incontinent bag lady came up to me, patted me on the arm and took the piss. 'My, I bet your parents are proud,' she smirked. It seems that I had sunk very low in the social hierarchy, below bag lady even.

DAN KIERAN

22 RODENT EXTERMINATOR

Hours:
8.30am-4.30am
Wages:
£1.25 per hour

DISGUSTING, IMMORAL

It was hopeless miscasting - a full-on animal rights activist and vegetarian getting paid to skulk around an airplane-hangar-sized shed stuffed with squawking, filthy, terrified chickens, looking for rats to kill.

My weapon was the latest advance in biological warfare (for 1980) , a hammer. How was I going to catch - let alone kill - a rat? I was at least four stone overweight and had no reserves of energy whatsoever. My only hope was if an arthritic, senile rat hobbled up to me and asked me to put him out of his misery. Suicidal rats with a good command of English are pretty thin on the ground, though.

After about fifteen minutes I'd had enough. I dropped the hammer and walked out into the autumn rain. The boss hollered to me as I trudged across the field, 'Wozza matter? You chicken or summink?' I couldn't even be bothered to figure out if he was intentionally trying to be funny.

BUFF ORPINGTON

21 WASHER-UPPER

Hours:
8.30am-6am
Wages:
Didn't get paid

DISGUSTING,
HUMILIATING

I once got suckered by a temp agency into going for a job as a kitchen porter in a hotel in Bournemouth. After a formal half-hour interview (why?), I was offered the job on the spot and told to start work straight away.

I was led into the kitchens and introduced to the other kitchen porter, who was a Scottish psychopath in his fifties who'd spent most of his adult life in prison for various violent crimes. He outlined the laborious tasks that were to befall me over the next couple of days - basically washing pots and pans.

This Scottish guy was a real pro kitchen porter. He'd apparently spent about twenty years in prison doing the job and consequently his hands

were like leather. He'd fill up the sink with water that was near boiling point and just stick his hands in it for hours. As there were no rubber gloves, I was expected to do the same. It was complete agony. If you winced at all he'd stare at you as if he was about to slash your throat, so I just persevered.

After two days my hands were completely blistered. I had one blister that was so painful that it brought tears to my eyes. When the Scottish bloke sloped off for a crap, I plucked up the courage and asked the Head Chef, who was also the owner of the Hotel, if he had a plaster. He reluctantly gave me one but told me if I needed another one it would be taken from my wages.

At that point I walked out. The temp agency wouldn't even pay me. A bad experience, but perhaps not as bad though as my friend who used to work in a porn shop in Soho. He spent six months in a dingy basement placing stickers over erections in European porn mags to meet British decency law restrictions. He also once had to clean out a customer's vibrating vagina that had stopped working because the mechanics had been caked in cum.

CRAIG LEE

20 GARLIC GRADER

Hours:
6am-6am
Wages:
£6 per hour

DISGUSTING,
DANGEROUS

It felt like the longest, hottest summer in recorded history. All my mates spent the summer reclining on the beach but I left home every morning at 6am to walk the six miles to my job at the garlic farm.

My co-workers were a dubious gang of imbeciles. (A number of them went on to better themselves; GBH and large-scale counter-feiting among some of their more colourful later achievements.) It was foul-smelling, back-breaking work in desert-storm conditions and if the agonizing heat didn't blister your skin, the blunt secateurs soon made mincemeat of your fingers.

I suppose I dreamt it would be dead French and romantic, passing the summer months getting back to nature, working in the fields, bronzed, dusty and physically exhausted by the end of each day, watching the sun set

over a glass of wine. Bollocks. There was a fight every other day, which tested your wits and agility if you inadvertently got caught in the crossfire. (The weapon of choice was the aforementioned secateur) And when these gimps weren't fighting they were trying to smoke the stuff.

Not only was garlic packing hard work for very little money - it stank. The warm garlic smell permeated my skin, every fibre of clothing and every strand of hair. However, this was just about tolerable compared to the gag-inducing stench emanating from the sweetcorn factory next door. We heard that you could earn a bit more there in return for jamming your thumbs into corn cobs to rid them of caterpillars. We gave it a go but lasted just one day - despite being in the company of an ex-rockstar who lunched alongside us. God knows how the poor man ended up in there.

The fella that owned the open-air sweatshop recently got done for using illegal chemicals on his land. My average earnings amounted to £6.00 a day.

SYLVIE POULTON

19 FEATURE FILM ANIMATOR

Hours:
9am-1am
Wages:
£4 per hour

SOUL-DESTROYING, FUTILE

I got a job on an animated feature in 1991, a personal project of a critically acclaimed animator. He had been gestating this thing since the seventies and had finally got a little Hollywood backing and hired a small, underpaid crew to give birth to his 'baby'. It was going to be the greatest animation feature of all time. The basic remit was to prove that he was the greatest animator who ever lived.

The feature was ludicrously complicated in design and detail. This added a rich layer of agony to what is already a bad business, for making animations is hellishly laborious. At twenty-four frames a second, it takes a crew of hundreds many months to produce the drawings you see on screen. Each animator

produces key drawings, their assistant draws the principal frames that lie between each key. This set of drawings is then passed to the in-betweener, whose job it is to fill in all the remaining frames, which, when filmed, will produce the illusion of fluid movement. I spent ten months drawing tiny incremental movements for upwards of 54 hours a week. We sat at our desks for up to 16 hours a day, the only sound the rasp of flicked paper and the 'tsk tsk' of personal stereos. The work was repetitive and minute. Each drawing could take up to an hour.

I hated the spirit-crushing work, I hated the endless hours and I disliked the people. Before web design, animators were the geeks of the creative industries. Some of my colleagues were strangely autistic: collectors of memorabilia from cartoons and TV science-fiction shows. Very few were married.

A few months after I was laid off, I was mooching around Colombia trying to feel better about myself when I caught a ride with a rich vacationing Ecuadorian couple. I explained about the film I had been working on and the laborious nature of animation feature production. The husband came up with a great description of the business, one that evokes the minuteness and accuracy and machine-like tedium, but also the grand collective effort.

'That's the work of ants,' he said.

STEVE HANDLEY

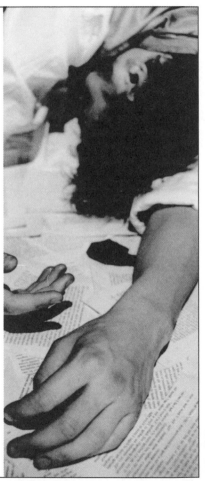

18 KOALA STUFFER

Hours:
7am-6am
Wages:
£1.10 per hour

DISGUSTING

I am still haunted by the memory of my day filling plastic koala bears with honey.

Australia, 1987. Stuck in Perth with no money and a broken-down van, I had no alternative. OK, it didn't sound as appealing as a day on the beach lying next to a board and pretending to be a surfer, but with thoughts of bee hives and flowers evoked, I said yes.

The bloke picked me up at 7am the next day, and explained we'd get 50 cents for every box of plastic koala bears we filled. There would be four of us, one to fill the koalas, one to screw the lids on, one to stick the labels on and one to pack them into boxes.

The factory was a small wooden hut, and we stood there for hours, screwing on lids, sticking on labels and packing boxes. But in our own way we were happy, at least until it was our turn to work the honey machine.

The honey had to be heated up to make it runny. Then it was pumped from a big vat out the back into a giant silver funnel. You sat below the funnel, using a foot pump to release bursts of honey into the plastic koalas. Simple, except that the honey was pumped into the funnel quicker than it could physically be released into the bears. There was a mirror above you so you could keep an eye on your honey level, and as soon as it got near the top you had to run round the back and switch off the pump. Except that you kept forgetting.

Just as you were finding a subconscious rhythm on the machine, the sweet stuff would hit you from above. The goo was merciless. You'd be buried in a sea of stickiness in seconds. Then it would keep on pumping all over you, all over the floor, under the doors and out on to the street, until someone got to the pump.

It took about an hour to clean up a dreaded honey overflow, and we lost several hours of production that day. In all I think I earned about £10. I cut short my trip and returned home, traumatized and slightly sticky. **JIM DREWETT**

17 SPY

**Hours:
Thirty years
Wages:
Classified**

SOUL-DESTROYING

After a glorious Oxbridge education my uncle started working for MI5 in 1952. His first assignment was to inflitrate the Communist Party. He was given a new name, a job working for the railways and the task of immersing himself in his new identity. After ten years he had worked his way up through the railworkers' union to a position of influence within the Communist Party, but his success was to be his downfall. He was such a good asset to MI5 that it became less and less likely that they would ever allow such a successful operative to 'come out' and be re-assigned to another mission.

He had to live on the Rail workers' salary so as not to draw attention to himself, he wasn't allowed to pursue any interests that might conflict with his identity, he couldn't have any time off from his 'new life' and had constantly to lie to his family. So throughout the next thirty years the only link he had with the intelligence service was a monthly meeting with his contact at MI5.

In the end he went mad, his wife and children left him and he started to compulsively collect newspaper clippings that related to his original mission. The piles of paper began to take over his house. It got so bad that in the end he had to cut pathways through the piles of newspaper that had filled every room. Eventually, because newspaper is made from poor quality paper, the paper dust he habitually inhaled began to shred his lungs with tiny paper cuts until one day he effectively 'drowned' in his own blood. The truth about his life only emerged ten years after he was buried.

Most crap jobs steal some of your time. His stole his life.

ANON

16 EDITORIAL ASSISTANT

Hours:
9am-6pm
Wages:
£7 per hour

HUMILIATING,
SOUL-DESTROYING

When I was offered a job working for a local newspaper as an Editorial Assistant, I thought this would be my chance to prove I could make it in the cut-and-thrust world of journalism.

At the interview, the Newsroom Editor, Mr X, spent most of the interview staring at my breasts with a huge grin on his face. He asked if I could type, I said, 'Not really,' he said, 'It doesn't matter,' and I'd got the job. I was so proud of myself.

The journalists were all fresh out of journalist school and we all got on very well (they had taken me under their alcoholic wings), but they all hated Mr X, said he was a complete arsehole and to watch out. I was responsible for typing in the news, sports results and the letters page.

This was all very well for a while and then one day I approached Mr X and asked what I would have to do to get on to the reporting side of things. Mr X laughed and said editorial assistants are editorial assistants and journalists spend a lot of time in college training for these jobs. I was aware of the education route but was also aware of an in-house training route that Mr X was not telling me about.

After that he asked if I fancied going for a drink and that maybe I could come over to his and we'd go out from there. I wanted to be sick. I declined the offer and went off with the trained boozers for a night of drunken debauchery.

Had I gone for that drink or met him at his house I suppose things might have been different, but I didn't and he soon turned very nasty.

The jobs got worse. I kept making errors with the sports results. Mr X would penalize me for this all the time, even though it wasn't entirely my fault as they were faxed through and black lines would appear through vital results.

In the end I made them up, and this made the job quite fun, 'Chilly Wanderers 50 - Cool Katz 0'. It all depended on the names. If I liked them, they would get more points. Evidently this proved how many people studied the results because I never had a complaint. These typos went on for a while, keeping me happy. The meaner Mr X was, the more mistakes I would make.

One day Mr X came storming over to my desk and said, 'Get in my office now!' He wasn't happy.

I went in and took a seat opposite him. This is where my job interview had taken place, but now he wasn't smiling or even looking at my breasts. His face was very red and he shoved an A4 memorandum under my nose and told me to read through it.

Memorandum
To: me
From: Mr X

A series of errors have been brought to my attention over the last two weeks which are of great cause of concern to me. These have brought considerable embarrassment to the paper.

Firstly - this week in the village news you typed the word 'provision' instead of 'prevention' in the sentence: 'The final

Football results

CHAMPIONS LEAGUE
Semi–final, first leg
Porto (0) 0   D Coruna (0) 0
50,818

PONTIN'S HOLIDAYS LEAGUE
Premier Division: Burnley 2 Preston 2; Sheff Wed 3 Rotherham 1.
First Division: Carlisle 2 Blackpool 1; Wigan 2 Oldham 2.

PONTIN'S HOLIDAYS INSURANCE LEAG
First Division East: Boston Utd 0 Donc 2; Lincoln 2 York 1; Scunthorpe 2 Grim

PONTIN'S HOLIDAYS LEAGUE CUP
Semi–final: Tranmere 2 Sheff Utd

PONTIN'S HOLIDAYS COMBIN
...st Division: Cardi ...rnemouth 2

decision on the future management of Hooney Island must ensure the long term prevention of flooding of Bompton Marsh and Great Field', changing its whole meaning.

Secondly, the word 'bee' was omitted in the sentence: 'The bee population in France is already disorientated by genetically modified maize'. The editor had to apologize in the next week's paper.

Thirdly and most seriously you changed the word 'Poppy' for 'Poopy' 'Mrs Cobblebottom laid a grand 'Poopy' wreath on the war memorial on behalf of the W.I.'

These mistakes, which are by no means the first, are unacceptable to the paper. Any further errors will leave me no option but to take further action.

I tried my hardest not to laugh at what I was reading but I couldn't help it. I fought to regain my composure but a snotty snort came out of my nose. It felt like my blood vessels were about to burst as I struggled to contain my growing hysteria. My shoulders were shaking and this made Mr X really angry. He shouted at me, 'This is not funny. You could destroy the paper's reputation.' I tried to calm him down by saying, 'Oh come on, you must see the funny side of it.' This made him really angry, and he gave me a verbal warning.

A few weeks later I was asked whether I wished to take redundancy. I couldn't believe my luck: I had retained my dignity, and got paid to leave.

I ran in to Mr X a few years later when I was offered a commission to make a sculpture for a company. I entered the office where I would meet with clients to discuss the sculpture, and there was Mr X. The beam had returned to his face, as he was now happily married with lots of kids. The rest of the staff told me he was still a twat.

ABIGAIL FALLIS

15 GERIATRIC NURSE

Hours:
9am-4pm
Wages:
£5 per hour

DISGUSTING, HUMILIATING

When I was eighteen I worked

at a nursing home. Most of the residents were ga-ga, all wore adult nappys and the only bloke in there died on my first weekend. I was responsible for feeding, toileting and cleaning. Feeding meant timing the cycle of grunts, figuring out when the mouth was at its widest and tongue at the lowest point, then shoving a spoon of pulverized food up into the roof of the mouth and withdrawing it so that the food remained behind the gum. Usually most of it would come out as the new cycle of groaning commenced.

Toileting and cleaning were normally done together. Whilst the old dear evacuated herself on the commode you were distracted from the death-metal odour by having to clean faces, armpits and ancient tits. I was terrified.

After the commode pan was removed and its delicious contents disposed of I would get to work on the nether regions. I was in denial at this stage and questioned the authority of the person that employed me. Surely this was illegal? On more than one occasion the granny hadn't fully finished doing her business when I was down there cleaning her bits with warm, soapy water. Not only have I had my shoes shat on, but also I have cradled turds that have suddenly dropped into my hands. It was only on the second day that I realized you were supposed to wear gloves.

I am emotionally scarred for ever and cannot look at old people without wincing. **JAMIE DWELLY**

14 DATABASE BUILDER

Hours:
8.30am–5pm
Wages:
£2.50 per hour

DISGUSTING, FUTILE

I got sent to a Housing Association in Manchester to set up a database of their fleet of company cars. The work was shit but the two women there to show me the ropes, Brenda and Jackie, were two of the funniest people I had ever encountered.

Brenda was a computer whizz, she had been on advanced Word and Excel courses and knew more short cuts than anyone. She was in charge of arranging computer training for staff. Jackie was in charge of payroll and liked to 'call a spade a spade, with no messin'. Both were obsessive about dieting. They didn't just talk about food though. 'Big Brenda' and Jackie talked about their husbands, their houses and their kids. Apparently, Jackie's last pregnancy with Darren had been a long, and heavy nine months. She reminisced about the hot summer nights spent sitting by an open window watching the baby move from one side of her tummy to the other ('all bloody night it was'). She talked openly about the pain and agony felt during a twenty-six-hour labour and how 'bloody, shittingly awful, if I'm honest' the whole thing was.

But her description of her body after the birth was what really put me off. Jackie talked endlessly about her postnatal piles 'they were like huge purple golf balls hanging out me arse... The midwife came round one day and said 'Lie on ya side there, Jack,' and she nearly fainted when she saw them they were that bad... Ooooooh, they hurt like hell, don't they Bren? Did you have them then, Bren? Most people say they're like a bunch of grapes, don't they? But mine were like this jar of big juicy fucking shallots! Agony, honestly, agony...'

The lasting effects of child birth weren't confined to her arse. Jackie's arches had fallen on her feet and having a baby had also left her with a fat bum, fat thighs, a big fat belly and wing fat at the top of her arms (she used to flap her arms and watch the fat waves all afternoon when she was bored). 'Don't have a baby,' she would warn me, 'or you'll end up just like me.'

RACHEL POULTON

13 GRAVEDIGGER

Hours: 7am-3pm
Wages: £6 per hour

DISGUSTING, DANGEROUS

I've been a grave digger for seven years. Now you can say, 'Why work in a really shitty job like that?' But it gets worse, it's a Jewish Cemetery so often this isn't their final resting place.

Many Jewish families want their late relatives exhumed and sent to Israel. It's hard digging up an old person - he's got no clothes, got no skin, it don't matter if he's been there ten, twenty years - you rot at your own rate depending on how rotten you've been.

The one I dug up yesterday was fucking rotten. The smell makes you say, 'Go away, don't come anywhere near me!' But I couldn't find the toes and the, er, minor parts. I'm sure you wouldn't tell no one... but I've got 'em at home in the cupboard. But the worst thing? Trying to lift up a skeleton with a shovel when the head falls off. Oh, and the leeches - they live in the water that collects down there - they get on you and you're trying to fight them off. They're not that big but they're ugly. But the smell! You might think you know putridity and vile smells but I tell you, you know nothing. You do not know the hideous smell of death.

In dust, we trust. We're all going to dust. That's why I like the job.

ALBIE

12 PARK WARDEN

Hours:
8am-6pm
Wages:
£2.70 per hour

DISGUSTING,
DANGEROUS

My crappest job ever was as a Seasonal Parks Assistant or 'Parkie' in Wales. My previous term's lectures on Saussurian semiotics had taught me that signifiers, or 'words', bore no relation to their signified counterparts, 'objects'. And here was living proof. The word 'park' bore no relation whatsoever to the burrs, caltrops, weedkilled dandelions, vandal-contorted slides, melted plastic litter bins and random tumuli of steelworks-slag-gone-to-seed at my workplace. This was a sylvan landscape populated by glue-sniffing borstal-escapees and abandoned joyride wrecks, where every piece of park furniture would tell us to 'fuck off', and the occasional tufts of grass piercing through a

THE WANK TANK

crust of Jack Russell excreta meant we had to mow, mow, mow all day long. A bit like that farmer character out of Bod.

The first week was spent with myself and another student-jobber devising effective techniques for bullying the park's most regular customer - a solitary, mackintoshed pervert in his late forties - to make him vacate his observation bench next to the children's play areas and retreat to the toilets (which we would later hose down and bleach). Of course, for this we earnt no thanks from the shellsuited, black-eyed, three-infants-and-counting teenage mums who spent entire afternoons in the children's area, screaming at their offspring as they gorged on Crunchies, Curly Wurlies and Monster Munch. Appalling ingratitude, but still.

The job seemed almost tolerable at this stage. With a little common sense we could avoid being spat on by local toughs, groped by lonely old ladies or mauled by skinhead-wielding pit-bull terriers. And what fun we parkies could have on our day-excursions to strim road verges and central reservations! By placing our Husqvarna strimmers at just the right angle, we could spray rain-soaked dogshit into each other's visors!

Just when we were about to ditch the two quid seventy an hour, my mate's sweep of the lockers in the parkies' hut revealed a stash of 1970s hardcore cockmags. We spent three entertaining tea breaks dissing a decade of bright pastel lingerie, botched shaven havens and those black censorship stars over jizzuming japs' eyes, the Danish-English captions denying all eroticism. 'Lick my klitty! Oo-oh that's hot!' and the like. This passed idle seconds until the head parkie found out that we'd found his stash and - far from showing any embarrassment - suggested he lend us his videos, which were 'really dirty', after that we re-christened his hut the 'wank-tank'. We'd more or less decided to head for the beach and penury when a new parkie joined the

team. Our workmate was a career dole-bludger on a DHSS back-to-work scheme known only as 'Des'. He would entertain us for entire minutes with stories of Swansea's darkside, such as his once having 'licked out' a stripper, who'd stuck a Marathon up her gange, before getting his beard 'all mingin, like' with her 'brown gash dripping with peanuts and chocolate'.

Then things got really weird.

First we were asked to work nights guarding turf. The council had laid £8,000 worth of turf on an old industrial wasteground ready for, if I remember, the national festival. But this was Wales and stolen turf could be fenced by local thieves. So the council needed someone to guard the grass overnight until it took root. We were selected because we were students and therefore the only parkies with fucked-up body clocks. Now it might seem a dream to get paid to watch grass grow, but it wasn't because we had to do this alone on alternate nights with no electricity. Cue three nights each of sitting in a portakabin, eating cheese-and-pickle sarnies, swearing as our Walkman batteries gave up at around midnight, and feeling scared that we would be beaten up by thieving junkies who might have been tipped off about the turf. Both of us admitted to strolling around the field shouting 'grow, grow, grow' at the grass. And Des had of course made our job merrier by twice asking his pisshead mates to drum on the back of the por-takabin at 3am.

Unfortunately, our being chosen for the grass job had pissed off a 'permanent' who'd wanted the job, so we were now targets for revenge. The following Thursday we were told to report to the cemetery with our strimmers. 'Excellent, more dogshit on visors!' we exclaimed. But when we got to the cemetery we were told that we had been signed up for a 're-opener', that is to dig

a grave for a coffin to be stacked on top of another. Not knowing how to dig graves, we were given a briefing by the gravedigger who was proud to have dug around 6,000 in his lifetime. We learnt that nowadays mechanical excavators are used for fresh graves, but for re-openers people still need to use spades and muscle other-wise they might damage the coffin. Anyhow, we made good progress, hitting the lid of the coffin beneath our feet by lunchtime, and being not a lit-tle freaked out that the nameplate on the coffin was still shiny after having being in the ground for thirty-odd years. We went to fetch our lunch, using the opportunity to search the gravedigger's cabin before returning to the grave (no necrophilia mags as we'd imagined, just more sev-enties Svens and Erikas and a bestiality playing card set). The sun was shining and we were almost enjoying our little *déjeuner sur cercueil* when Kev, a trainee parkie with an old white bodykitted XR3, turned up 'to help'. Everybody hated Kev. And Kev's 'help', after digging out a few clods of earth we'd left behind, involved wanting to open the coffin to see 'what people look like when they're dead'. We just sat at the edge of the fresh-dug and looked down in disbe-lief at this cretin's attempts to crowbar the cof-fin-lid. By this time, a big funeral party had arrived at the end of our row to bury a member of the local male voice choir. Kev couldn't see this hap-pening as he was crowbarring away at the edge of the coffin lid. He obviously wasn't too bright otherwise he would have realized that by standing on the coffin lid, he was exerting downward pressure on the lid and he couldn't open it up. Anyhow, to our surprise he dropped the crowbar and started pogoing on top of the spade on top of the coffin - whack, whack, whack. CRACK. The funeral party suddenly burst into 'Guide Me O Thou Great Redeemer'. The last thing I remember was Kev in epileptic spasms atop the coffin, wondering what the fuck he had released. We never did see the corpse.

SIWMAE

11 SIGMOIDOSCOPE CLEANER

Hours:
9am-5pm
Wages:
£7.50 per hour

DISGUSTING, HUMILIATING

The worst job I had was in the sterile supplies department of a large London hospital. I had to clean out Sigmoidoscopes. For those of you that don't know, Sigmoidoscopes are used for looking up people's bums and were unsurprisingly usually covered in shit. The room was unbearably hot and steamy and stank to high heaven. You'd had a good day if you managed not to get a hypodermic syringe stuck in your finger and hadn't had a placenta drop on to your shoes. Somehow I managed to stick it out for three months.

MANDY

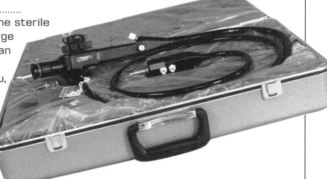

CRAP JOB TRIVIA

PIG TRIVIA
A pig's penis is shaped like a corkscrew and its orgasm can last up to half an hour.

10 PIG WANKER

Hours:
8am-4pm
Wages:
£6.50 per hour

DISGUSTING,
HUMILIATING, IMMORAL

I worked at a fast food restaurant in Liverpool. I didn't get any stars. I failed all the tests, even though they merely involved copying the answers from the fast food restaurant's Test Answers into the questionnaire. Also, I had to work twice as hard as a few of the other staff who were junkies and couldn't be trusted to operate the deep fat fryer. They were very good at cleaning, though. They could polish one square yard of stainless steel for eight hours. Meticulous, if not efficient.

As bad as this was, I have to say it beats working in an office any day. Even standing on the gangplank of a ship for twelve hours while working as a security guard at Seaforth docks was better than bleaching my mind by staring into a monitor for a decade.

When I think about it, I once met the man with the worst job in the world. I was at a party and he was introduced to me as a 'pig wanker'. That is, he manually stimulated pigs until they filled a beaker with their issue. I said, 'Let me shake you by the hand.'

MDA

9 CIVIL SERVANT

Hours:
9am-7pm
Wages:
£8 per hour

DISGUSTING,
SOUL-DESTROYING

Moving down to London straight after university, me and my friends soon discovered the streets were paved with syringes, empty spooky brew cans and chicken bones. Setting ourselves up in a hole in Lewisham, we lived a simple life - passing the time by scouring the Monday *Guardian* Jobs section, crying ourselves to sleep and avoiding pitched Yardie gang battles.

Me and the lads raised our self-esteem by taking temping jobs. We all had our highpoints, from recording data about the bits left over after medical operations, to dressing up in a huge inflatable mobile phone to hand out leaflets.

My own personally tailored stygian creek was a strip-lit dungeon in Westminster. There I would take phone calls from the hierarchically obsessed government staff, 'my number five has asked me to point out that there is a plant that needs watering next to the sink on the fifth floor', or more intriguingly, 'my number two says that the toilets are out of paper in the second-floor Men's'. I would then have to phone either the janitor or the odd job man to see if they could be arsed to do the job.

The thing I came to realize is that it's actually a rather clever ruse for cutting down employment figures - the government employ the unemployable. One fine example of 'care in the workplace' could not be burnt out of my memory even after years of counselling: 'Fearsome Graham'. Fearsome Graham would wander around the building handing out post. However, he believed that one of the perks of his job was to wander about without his trousers or pants on, and rush into the toilets to watch you while you were trying to urinate.

Still I did get to learn of the Senior Tory MP who was a little too regular in his morning routine. Everyday he would use the same toilet cubicle at the same hour.

The fire service had to be called as it appears that someone had accidentally left some superglue on the toilet seat. The file reported that three men had to yank him off, leaving remnants of 'hair and skin'.

DANNY BOBBECK

8 CREDIT CARD SALESMAN

Hours:
8.30am-5.30pm
Wages:
£6.50 per hour

SOUL-DESTROYING, IMMORAL

I have had many jobs - isn't that always the case? But the bank I worked for who delighted in issuing credit cards to poor people with bad debts proved to be the worst of them by a mile.

As I drove into the wanky world of the out-of-town business park I quickly realized that there were no pubs, and the park was strategically positioned more than fifteen minutes' drive from any friendly inn. I drove my Fiesta alongside the Audi TTs through the heartland of shimmering corporate edifices. Slowly the jewel in the capitalist play-pen rose across the horizon, a faux Georgian monstrosity that housed my new employer. I later learnt that this place had a voracious appetite that was capable of devouring over 4,500 souls and it was hungry for mine.

On entering, I was ruthlessly checked for explosives and had to sign over fifteen forms that incriminated me in advance for everything, from not flushing the chain, through to blowing the company up. I spent the next eight hours being led around its pristine corridors by an overweight plebeian called Sarah who had less intelligence than an amoeba. When I asked her polite questions she found it difficult to process anything resembling a sentence and instead let her gravy-filled head loll about insouciantly on its fat neck.

Above every door, of which there were many, the words 'Think of yourself as the customer' were inscribed in gold lettering. The walls of the main corridor, off which the phone pens were situated, were adorned with portraits of the fools who had already given up five years of their lives to kissing corporate yankee arse. Once you had achieved this goal your badge was upgraded to one with a star. The star badge entitled the owners to the best parking spaces, personal chefs and free fags. Well, not quite, but the inequality was considerable.

The job involved little more than upsetting the exploited customers, to whom the company had maliciously issued credit cards. This was boring and very stupid - as is often the case with the phone monkey sector. We could rarely help the customer, and were forbidden to agree that the company had fucked them over. I had moral problems with this, and eventually took it upon myself to tell as many customers as possible to cut up their cards if they couldn't afford them. My friend and I worked out that if we had done just that for the next forty-five years we would have only diminished their customer base by 2%.

NICHOLAS COOKE

CRAP JOBS

7 POSTMAN

Hours:
Mon-Fri 6.15am-3pm
Sat 6.15am-11.15am
Wages:
£9.86 per hour

SOUL-DESTROYING

I should be happy. Instead of
two deliveries a day, Royal Mail
now only have a single delivery
service. Plus, we only work five
days a week now instead of six.
Plus! Plus! Plus! We now get an
extra £25 a week.

I should be happy, but I'm not.

Neither is anyone else. The areas we deliver to
have doubled in size (because the number of
delivery offices have halved), which means it
takes twice as long to sort each morning's K2-
sized mountain of mail; which means people are
getting their mail at least three hours later than
before; which means postmen are getting their
lugs caned by an irate populace screaming,
'Where are my air tickets? I'm supposed to be
going to Gran Canaria tomorrow' and suchlike;
which means I'm finishing work later than ever, so
when I stagger back through my front door all I
want is a warm bed or a quick death.

The extra day off is spent in a semi-comatose
condition, my legs fucked like rank gorgonzola

144

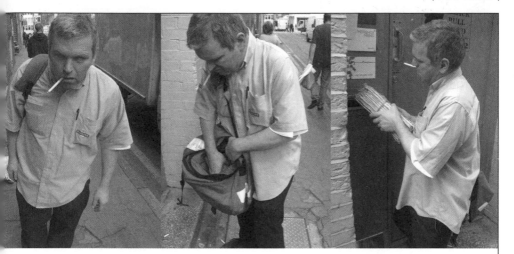

cornets. As for the extra £25 per week - that's our old £100 monthly bonus quartered.

The sense of camaraderie has vanished. With so much work on our hands the time for friendships and jabbers over a snout of lungpuncher is no more. No tea breaks, no lunches, just work, work, fucking work with a side order of work and a strawberry workshake.

If the soul-killing, grinding monotony and fun-lessness of the new regime isn't intolerable enough, I have to endure the vapid mind-destroying drones of London radio station Magic FM blasting away at me all morning. (What's so magic about Magic FM? The fact they miraculously play the same bloody maudlin ballads every bastard morning?) They should rename it, Divorce FM. Elton John's 'Sacrifice', Phil Collins' 'Against All Odds', Chicago's 'If You Leave Me Now', 'Lionel Bloody Richie's 'Three Times a Lady', ARGHHH!

Being a postman now is like living through *Groundhog Day* and Magic FM is the perfect soundtrack album.

IAN REDDIE

6 TRAINEE SOLICITOR

Hours:
8.30am-9pm
Wages:
£9.50 per hour

HUMILIATING,
SOUL-DESTROYING

So desperate was I to get a foot on the legal ladder that I accepted a paralegal job at a local solicitor's for minimum wage. My sense of fair play being what it is, I decided to do as little work as humanly possible in return. However, my boss had other ideas. If she was going to pay me minimum wages she was determined to treat me like any other minimum-wage-slave, and give me any and every shitty task she could think of. After about a month of fighting spiders the size of my head in the 'archives' (153,000 unlabelled boxes stuffed full of random papers), repairing photocopiers (ever tried to remove a split toner cartridge when wearing a white shirt?), washing cars and, I kid you not,

cleaning shoes, I finally got a chance to join her in court, and do what I was trained to do. Luckily my college had trained me very well at sitting quietly and taking notes, as that was about the limit of my duties. I'd start taking notes at about 10.30am, finish at 4pm, then spend the evening writing them up into something vaguely comprehensible. This was apart from the day my boss arrived about three hours late, leaving me to calm a hysterical client who was about to see her children taken into care and pacify a furious judge

who clearly didn't appreciate the fact that the delay was eating into his afternoon on the links.

The final nail in the coffin came a couple of weeks later. The one saving grace about the job was that every day at 2pm sharp, the boss would give me £20 and send me to the local off-licence to get her '40 Lambert & Butler, and two of the cheapest bottles of white wine they've got. And get yourself a few cans if you want.' Several hours into one such session, she stopped dictating a letter to me mid sentence and exited the room hastily. My career path was settled the second I noticed the substantial dark patch on the chair on which she had been sitting. Lousy tasks for no money I could handle, but incontinence was above and beyond the call of duty. I was out of the door before she'd returned from the bathroom. For all I know she's still in there...

BILL HANDLEY

5 RECRUITMENT CONSULTANT

Hours:
Mon-Fri 8am-5pm
Wages:
£9 per hour

SOUL-DESTROYING, IMMORAL

I was set to work hiring staff for a large call centre. The jobs were mind-numbingly repetitive and badly paid. Plus, due to the 24-hour, seven days-a-week society we insist on living in, they all had punishing long shifts.

Initially I was able to employ every druggie sociopath in the city. However, things soon took a turn for the worse and instead of hiring, my role was reversed. Because all employees were on temporary contracts, all could be made redundant on a manager's whim, and so the bosses preyed on the defenceless like a pack of shabby, feral cats. One person rang complaining of being ill - sacked; another went to the vending machine at the wrong time - sacked another late back from lunch - sacked.

I had to forcefully remove their ID badges and get security to boot them out the door. I was given the nickname 'The Undertaker' as I cut a swathe through the company. Eventually, having sacked twenty people in one day the manager called me into his office to inform me that I was sacked too. What goes around comes around.

ADAM J. SHARDLOW

4 NIGHT PETROL STATION CASHIER

Hours:
10pm-6am
Wages:
£6.50 per hour

DANGEROUS, DISGUSTING,
HUMILIATING, SOUL-DESTROYING

Working at a petrol station by day is a deeply unsatisfying endeavour. When someone picks up a pump a beeper goes off and you press a button. That's it. Working nights at a petrol station is my vision of hell. You're locked in. There's no escape. You're made to feel like a terminally bored zoo exhibit, you share your evening with the hum of fluorescent lights, the smell of petrol and - the customers.

Dear God, the customers.

After 11 o'clock nobody wants petrol except taxi drivers. After 11 o'clock the fun starts. You probably recognize the following scenario. You've probably been in it. You've probably been the person who wants to know what sandwiches I've got. I don't have any fucking sandwiches but nonetheless I'll check what's in the shop. After making my way round the counter and shouting out all fourteen varieties of chicken sandwich, you have probably replied that you no longer require a sandwich and would rather have some AA batteries instead.

You bastard.

I hated you. Not as much as the customers who threatened to come and twat me when the doors were opened, but I still hated you. Even hairy, hairy Jesus would have lost his patience had he been forced to hunt down snack foods and dairy products all through the night. Of course there was more to the job. I had to contend with dodgy scallies trying out their new stolen credit cards, those doing runners after filling up, and those who fling bottles and bags of coal around the forecourt. There were also the nightly thrills of the two-hour stock-take and floor mopping.

After a few months of enduring this tedium I got fired for 'inaction'. Some pissed-up knuckle-scraper pulled the cover off one of the pumps, leaving bits of it all over the forecourt and obviously rendering it
inactive. Apparently, I should have reported this incident to the police. I didn't though, and got fired. Thank God.

JOHN McCAFFREY

3 IT MANAGER

Hours:
8am-7pm
Wages:
£20 per hour

SOUL-DESTROYING,
HUMILIATING, FUTILE

Unperturbed by my lack of academic brilliance, I managed to have a career with a computer company for over thirty years. My 'career' rose, ebbed, swelled and contracted as prescribed by the influences of the various shades of managerial dysfunction. Some managerial styles were based on free gifts, others on appraisal and yet other variants on fear. But the crunch really came when my department was bought by a smaller, business-focused organization. Under the new regime, this aging idler stood out like a sore thumb. Once the honeymoon was over, I found that I had been named in an email to every employee as the person behind some project that went belly-up.

Suffice to say that I was not culpable so I shrugged off this slur and went about my duties as before. All about me, like those knocks at the door once so prevalent in Russia under Beria or the disappeared of Argentina, people began to leave the company. One day you shared a project, the next they'd disappeared! Targets not met, opposition to policy? The seemingly wise and secure, gradually got targeted. The gloves were off!

It took no genius to work out that the company did not sack people; it frightened them away, threatened them away or whispered them out of existence.

Had I been a Prussian officer or a Samurai I could have found solace with my ancestors but, rather than face the stigma of constantly being named, shamed and excluded, I decided to give in to my natural instincts and have a nervous breakdown. I collapsed into a heap of remorse, self-vilification and thoughts of mortality.

The day before I gave up on this chapter of my life I went to see the boss.

'You don't want me here, do you?'

No response.

'Can't you see what an awful state I'm in?'

No response.

'Would you consider making me redundant.'

Suddenly, the man found his voice. He would ask the partners. There are many ways of killing people in the naked city, this is just one of them. I now play my lute and write furiously, and the rest of the time I am King Lear's fool. Oh happy days! **MALCOLM TURNER**

2 NORTH SEA FERRY CABIN CLEANER

Hours:
5am-7pm (including
2 hours of breaks)
Wages:
£3 per hour

DISGUSTING, HUMILIATING,
SOUL-DESTROYING

I spent a summer working as cabin crew for a North Sea ferry company, running to a large port in Holland, on a huge, 33,000 ton floating hotel. Attached to the Hotel Services Department, my job was to clean cabins. The ship in question carries some 1600 passengers, and in the summer has well over 200 crew, most of whom are students and other young carefree types who enjoyed the party lifestyle on board. We all had our own cabins, and lived on the ship, sharing a bathroom with one other cabin. You make a lot of friends and have a really good time, but it does definitely have a downside. You get up at 4.15am all dressed and ready for work - the outfit included dark-grey wool trousers, a white shirt, clip-on blue tie, and a green waitcoat, with steel-toecap shoes. You meet in the crew mess for a coffee and head off down to seven deck to begin cleaning the cabins. The passengers are roused from their slumber at five by the PA system, and asked nicely to get up and out so we can clean the cabins ready for the next lot. We always did the seven deck cabins first, as they were exclusively for the freight drivers. This involved stripping sheets, duvet covers and pillow cases off the two bunkbeds (whether they had been slept in or not), putting clean sheets on, hoovering the carpet, and making the bathroom spotless with sprays and cloths. And all inside four minutes. This feat was repeated for the 450-plus four-berth cabins on the ship during the course of the day. If we had a full load the previous night, we would be cleaning cabins all day, and finish just in time to clean the freight drivers' cabins in preparation for the 8:30pm night sailing. When we had a light load we would finish by midday.

At night, despite strict drinking and drugs laws to the contrary, we would all pile into one of the crew cabins and get slaughtered on the duty free grog we'd bribed a freight driver to buy for us. There were more girls than geezers and, needless to say, in

the absence of DVDs, Playstations and good TV, there were lots and lots and LOTS of sexual relationships going on: three, four, five in a bed - you name it, it all went on. There was a good game where we all piled into a cabin and turned the lights off. Risky, but fun. They fed us three square meals a day, the same food as we gave the fares downstairs, and the money was excellent - worked out at about £80 a day.

But before you run off in search of this dream holiday job let me tell you why this was the most horrible job in the world. The British freight drivers were fine, and by and large, continent. Their continental brethren, on the other hand, thought nothing of taking a shit in the other bed, then covering it over with the sheets as a nice surprise for the cabin crew in the morning. They used to wet the bed, and move to another bed rather than walk the six paces to the toilet. They left their eye-watering Dutch animal porn in the rooms for us to find. They also made themselves sick in the effort to sober up from the dozen pints of ale and a curry consumed in the bar, before they took their 38 tonners out on the public roads. But they wouldn't do it in the bathroom where we could rinse it off with the shower. Oh no. They would chunder all over the room, and all over the soft furnishings. They would even throw up in the bin, then hurl it all over the beds and carpet just to be bloody minded. Arseholes. Bear in mind also that 450-plus cabins equates to maybe 300 separate pools of sick to be cleaned up if it blows anything more than a force five, which it normally does.

Then there was the British travelling public, who are notoriously bad travellers. I remember a Welsh family of three married couple, and a five-year-old boy. They were first up the stairs from the car deck once we commenced embarkation on a night sailing. The kid was green. He tugged at his mother's coat and said, 'Mum, I don't feel very well...' The mother clipped the infant round the ear and told him to shut up, while her morose husband asked me where their cabin was. At which point the child disappeared in an eruption of multicoloured vomit. I mean the kid just exploded. Apparently, said infant had consumed an entire family pack of Skittles, a banana and what looked like it might have been a pork pie or similar, during the drive down from Gwent. It was beautiful, in the same way that an atomic bomb cloud is beautiful but the problem was two fold, it was all over me, and my trousers and both parents, but not on the child. And it was on the area at the top of the main staircase from which a further 1597 passengers would soon trudge in the next twenty minutes. And it reeked. I looked around - none of my colleagues were anywhere to be seen.

But that doesn't seem too bad, does it? You still want the job? Let me tell you about another morning when my deck supervisor, another cabin crew member and I walked up the stairs to do the, 'slightly roomier family cabins' on ten deck. Our noses began to twitch on the eight deck stairs. By ten deck, the last of the passengers were scurrying past us, ashen faced, towards the car decks. And there was this smell. You know, that sickly smell you sometimes get in the butcher's shop? Smelt like that. Eventually, we narrowed the search down to one cabin. Even the eleven deck crew had come down to see what the unholy stench was about. The closer we got to cabin 1016 the more pungent and retch-some the smell became. We opened the door, and the wave of stench hit us like a freight train. Two of the five onlookers, including myself, threw up on the spot. Once I had finished blowing my break-fast I took in the scene before me. There was liquid shit everywhere. On the carpets. On all four of the beds, and inside them too. On the walls. On the curtains. Bemusingly, on the ceiling and windows. There was literally gallons of it. It looked like someone had got three pressure washers, one filled with diarrhoea, one with puke and one with something REALLY horrible, that was nei-ther one nor the other, and then cut loose on the room. For a long time. Bags of shop-ping and clothes lay all over the place, and one silver Nike Air Max trainer lay forlorn and alone on the floor almost filled with shit. The bathroom was indescribable. I could not stop retching. Just this clinging stench of rotten eggs, off milk, foul cheese and butchered meat that stung your eyes. I threatened indus-trial action if I was forced to clean it up, and so the decision was taken to rip out everything from the room - mattresses, curtains, carpet, floor tiles, then pour a whole bottle of carpet cleaner on the floor and to stuff towels under the door. We never used that cabin again until the ship went for refit in December.

ANON

1 PHONE SEX-LINE OPERATOR

Hours:
Midnight-6am
Wages:
£9 per hour

DANGEROUS, FUTILE, SOUL-DESTROYING, HUMILIATING, IMMORAL, DISGUSTING

Probably the only office-based job there is in which exclaiming, 'I don't want to be stuck in anal sex all day' won't be met by even the merest elevation of an eyebrow. After three months, however, the novelty had well and truly worn off. I had fodded wank one too many times and 'Fuckhead Syndrome' (the technical term for headaches and faintness caused by repeatedly faking orgasms) had set in. I had had enough of sitting on those dubiously damp wheelie-chairs in the domination department and enough of being punished for being late by having to stay in the anal sex chair for the duration of my shift. I had to leave.

It was a grubby office, which despite the physical absence of men, had a definite odour of spunk. (This might have been some sort of clever marketing ploy, like supermarkets pumping out the smell of baking bread and freshly ground coffee.) On my first day I was given my very own partitioned desk and phone-sex manual. This manual, I have to say, was a hugely entertaining tome, but sadly it has since been confiscated by Malaysian Customs and Excise officers. It contained gems such as 'Phrases Men Like to Hear From You', with 'I'm separating my arse cheeks' in the top ten. Also there was an excellent 'Dictionary of Filth', scripts for 'Lesbian Watersports' and a 'Guide for The Dominatrix'. From my own personal experience I can tell you that slaves like to be penetrated by stiletto heels; to be instructed to beat their own cocks with the telephone receiver; to have cigarettes stubbed out on their bollocks and to be severely punished when they inevitably jizz in your fishnet stockings after you specifically tell them not to. Incidentally, a dominatrix is up a little bit in the whole phone sex office hierarchy. You graduate to domination once you have done a few weeks on straight phone sex chitchat and endured the anal inauguration.

It is quite shocking how this all very quickly becomes mundane. Before you know it you are silencing entire restaurants and tube carriages with your hilari-

ON MY FIRST
DAY I WAS
GIVEN MY
VERY OWN
PARTITIONED
DESK AND
PHONE—SEX
MANUAL

I'm hot and ready for your call...

Just eighteen and horny as hell

I love short, bald men with bellies

0000 000 000

ous work-related anecdotes whilst friends and
family look on open-mouthed. After a while someone says, 'You've changed, you used to be such a
nice girl but now you're weird and perverted and
all you ever talk about is strap-on dildos, mutual
masturbation and separating your arse cheeks,
and I don't like having to call you "Mistress"'. And
you say, 'Oh crumbs Mum! You're right. I'd better
jack this in.' Most people don't last more than a
few months for this reason but incredibly I met
some women who had been doing it for six years
or more. They are serious Fuckheads, doing
double shifts, seven days a week, dribbling into
their headsets, tugging at their
gussets, rubbing their fat
thighs together, simultaneously chain-smoking and stuffing
their slack-jaws with Eccles
cakes whilst some weirdo
spends a pound a minute
telling them that in his excite-
ment he's ruined his carpet –
bizarre.   SARAH JANES

INDEX

SUBSCRIBE TO THE IDLER
SAVE MONEY · SAVE EFFORT · GET FREE THINGS

If you subscribe now, you'll save up to 22% on The Idler's cover price and we'll send you a snail tattoo and your own Grand Order of Idlers certificate

YES! I WOULD LIKE TO SUBSCRIBE TO THE IDLER FOR:

☐ 4 ISSUES AT JUST £40 – SAVE £8 (20%) OR

☐ 8 ISSUES AT JUST £75 – SAVE £21(22%)   TICK IF THIS IS A GIFT: ☐

SEND THIS SUBSCRIPTION TO:

MR/MS/MRS/MISS _____   ADDRESS: _____

_____

POSTCODE: _____

YOUR DETAILS (IF DIFFERENT FROM ABOVE):

MR/MS/MRS/MISS _____   ADDRESS: _____

_____

POSTCODE: _____

TOTAL AMOUNT* £ _____   PAID BY: ☐ CHEQUE (TO 'THE IDLER') ☐ VISA, MASTERCARD, AMEX, SWITCH:

CARD NO: ☐☐☐☐ ☐☐☐☐ ☐☐☐☐ ☐☐☐☐ ☐☐☐☐

EXPIRES: ☐☐☐☐   ISSUE NO. ☐ (SWITCH ONLY) SECURITY CODE ☐☐☐ (LAST 3 DIGITS ON SIGNATURE STRIP)

SIGNED: _____   YOUR E-MAIL ADDRESS: _____

*POSTAGE: prices quoted include postage in the UK. For the rest of Europe, add £8 per 4 issues, for the rest of the world, add £15 per 4 issues

TO SUBSCRIBE GO TO WWW.IDLER.CO.UK, CALL 020 7691 0319 OR FILL OUT AND SEND
THIS FORM TO: The Idler, Freepost, 24–28A Hatton Wall, London EC1B 1JA